MENDELSSOHN

Books by David Whitwell

Philosophic Foundations of Education
Foundations of Music Education
Music Education of the Future
The Sousa Oral History Project
The Art of Musical Conducting
The Longy Club: 1900–1917
A Concise History of the Wind Band
Wagner on Bands
Berlioz on Bands
Chopin: A Self-Portrait
Schumann: A Self-Portrait in His Own Words
La Téléphonie and the Universal Musical Language
Extraordinary Women
Aesthetics of Music in Ancient Civilizations
Aesthetics of Music in the Middle Ages
Aesthetics of Music in the Early Renaissance

The History and Literature of the Wind Band and Wind Ensemble Series

Volume 1 The Wind Band and Wind Ensemble Before 1500
Volume 2 The Renaissance Wind Band and Wind Ensemble
Volume 3 The Baroque Wind Band and Wind Ensemble
Volume 4 The Wind Band and Wind Ensemble of the Classical Period (1750–1800)
Volume 5 The Nineteenth-Century Wind Band and Wind Ensemble
Volume 6 A Catalog of Multi-Part Repertoire for Wind Instruments or for Undesignated Instrumentation before 1600
Volume 7 Baroque Wind Band and Wind Ensemble Repertoire
Volume 8 Classical Period Wind Band and Wind Ensemble Repertoire
Volume 9 Nineteenth-Century Wind Band and Wind Ensemble Repertoire
Volume 10 A Supplementary Catalog of Wind Band and Wind Ensemble Repertoire
Volume 11 A Catalog of Wind Repertoire before the Twentieth Century for One to Five Players
Volume 12 A Second Supplementary Catalog of Early Wind Band and Wind Ensemble Repertoire
Volume 13 Name Index, Volumes 1–12, The History and Literature of the Wind Band and Wind Ensemble

www.whitwellbooks.com

MENDELSSOHN: A SELF-PORTRAIT IN HIS OWN WORDS

David Whitwell

Whitwell Publishing: Austin, Texas, USA

Mendelssohn: A Self-Portrait In His Own Words
Second Edition
Dr. David Whitwell

WHITWELL PUBLISHING
815-A BRAZOS ST. #491
AUSTIN, TX 78701
WWW.WHITWELLPUBLISHING.COM

© 1986, 2012 by David Whitwell
All rights reserved. First edition 1986.
Second edition 2012

Composed in Bembo Book.
Published in the United States of America.
All images used in this book are in the public domain except where otherwise noted.

ISBN-13: 978-1-936512-50-8
ISBN-10: 1936512505

Contents

Foreword ix

A Brief Chronology of the Life of Felix Mendelssohn xi

Source Abbreviations xiii

Part I: Mendelssohn's Reflections on his own Music

Chapter One: Mendelssohn's General Outlook On Music 3

Chapter Two: Mendelssohn on his own Musical Studies 13

Chapter Three: Mendelssohn on his Creative Process 15

    Mendelssohn's Search for and Opera Libretto 25

Chapter Four: Mendelssohn on his own Compositions 29

Part II: Mendelssohn's View of the World of Music

Chapter Five: Mendelssohn's Observations on Performance and Performers 49

    On Pianoforte Playing 50

    On Singing 53

    On Opera 57

    On Orchestras 58

Chapter Six: Mendelssohn's Views on the Musical Characteristics of Various Countries 61

    Austria 61

    England 62

    France 63

    Germany 65

    Italy 71

    Switzerland 76

Chapter Seven: Mendelssohn's Views of the Public 77

Chapter Eight: Mendelssohn's Views of Criticism 79

Chapter Nine: Mendelssohn's Views on the Personalities of his Day 81

    Auber 81

    Bach 82

    Beethoven 83

    Berlioz 84

    Cherubini 85

    Chopin 86

    Czerny 88

    Ferdinand David 88

    Donizetti 88

    Gade 89

    Goethe 90

    Joachim 91

    Kalkbrenner 91

    Liszt 92

    Fanny Mendelssohn 93

    Meyerbeer 93

    Moscheles 94

    Mozart 94

    Neukomm 95

    Paganini 96

    Rossini 96

    Schubert 97

    Clara Schumann 97

    Robert Schumann 97

    Spohr 98

    Spontini 98

    Thalberg 99

    Queen Victoria 99

    Wagner 101

Part III: Mendelssohn: A Self-Portrait

Chapter Ten: Mendelssohn on his Personality and Character Traits 105

Chapter Eleven: Mendelssohn on his Physical and Mental Health 115

Chapter Twelve: Mendelssohn Describes his Experience as a Performer 125
    As a Piano Soloist 125
    As an Organist 130
    As a Conductor 132

Chapter Thirteen: Insights into Mendelssohn General Outlook on Life 137
    Nature 142
    Faith 143
    Time 144
    Women 145
    Teaching 146
    Painting 152
    Literature 153

Chapter Fourteen: Mendelssohn on his Daily and Professional Life 155

FOREWORD

This volume is not intended to be the traditional kind of autobiography, which all too often relegates the reader to the role of one on the side-line who can only observe the procession of dates, people, and facts which define the life of the subject. The purpose of the present volume is quite different. Here we will pass by the usual parade of events and happenings of Mendelssohn's life (excepting the brief chronological sketch below) and concentrate instead on his own thoughts, as expressed in his own words.

The purpose has been to bring together Mendelssohn's thoughts, drawn from many years and a variety of sources, and to present his thoughts chronologically by subject, to permit the reader insights into Mendelssohn's thinking on a subject and the development of these thoughts as they surface during his lifetime.

Apart from selecting subjects which would be of interest to the modern reader, the actual selection of the material herein has been limited to only those comments by Mendelssohn which seem to offer revelation on the man and his music. For example, not every reference to a particular composition has been included, but rather only those which might offer the reader an insight into how Mendelssohn himself viewed that composition.

With the hope of allowing the reader the most direct possible relationship with this master composer, I have resisted the strong and constant urge to add connecting or amplifying text and have left Mendelssohn's own thoughts to speak for themselves. My own experience in reading this material has been that I have felt a much closer relationship with Mendelssohn the man, something I somehow never quite achieved from traditional accounts of this master and his music. It is my hope that perhaps the reader as well might enjoy this experience.

A BRIEF CHRONOLOGY OF THE LIFE OF FELIX MENDELSSOHN

Felix Mendelssohn was born in 1809 into a cultivated German family, the grandfather, Moses, having been an important philosopher of the Enlightenment. Family connections, in part, helped provide the young composer with a broad education and acquaintances with important persons of the day, not the least of whom was Goethe.

The genius of Mendelssohn appeared early: at a very young age he had completed a large number of compositions, including the *A Midsummer Night's Dream* and *Meeresstille* Overtures, and had conducted the famous revival of Bach's *St. Matthew Passion*. The period of 1829–1833 saw the young composer broadening both his education and his reputation through extensive travel, to England, Italy, Switzerland, and Austria.

In 1833 Mendelssohn was appointed city music director in Düsseldorf, followed by his most important appointment as conductor of the Leipzig Gewandhaus Orchestra. Here, from 1835 to 1840, Mendelssohn was able to give full expression to his many talents as composer, pianist, and conductor. As conductor he promoted the works of other German composers, among them Schumann, in addition to the revival of numerous earlier compositions.

The final six years of his life included frequent travel, the frustrations of negotiating with officials in Berlin relative to a prospective position with the court there, and the satisfaction of helping to found the Leipzig Conservatory.

His early death, the anti-Semitic forces in Germany between 1850–1945, and the fact that his music looked back to Classicism more than ahead to Romanticism have all contributed to the relatively few performances of this great master's music heard today.

An especially personal description of Mendelssohn was published by his friend Eduard Devrient, which I believe the reader might enjoy:

> [Mendelssohn was] of middle height, slender frame, and of uncommon muscular power, a capital gymnast, swimmer, walker, rider, and dancer, the leading feature of his outward and inner nature was an extraordinary sensitiveness. Excitement stimulated him to the verge of frenzy, from which he was restored only by his sound, death-like sleep. This restorative he had always at hand; he has assured me that he had but to find himself alone and unoccupied in a room where there was a sofa, to go straightway to sleep. His brain had from childhood been taxed excessively, by the university course, study of modern languages, drawing, and much else,

and to these were added the study of music in its profoundest sense. The rapidity with which he mastered a score; his perfect understanding of the requirements of new compositions, the construction and complications of which were at once transparent to him; his marvelous memory, which placed under his hand the entire range of great works; these wondrous gifts filled me with frequent doubts as to whether his nervous power could possibly sustain him through the length of an ordinary life.

He never assumed to criticize on matters of taste, every kind of pretension being foreign to his nature. He hated all unrealness, affectation, and frivolity, as so much want of principle. This conscientiousness unmistakably ruled his musical faculty; he was thoroughly in earnest about all he did; the sense of duty was ever present to him, and forbade his offering to the world anything void of purpose, or for the mere sake of pleasing, anything immature or frivolous, much less anything vulgar, for the artist is bound to advance good taste and pure perception in his art.

SOURCE ABBREVIATIONS

Eduard Devrient, *My Recollections of Felix Mendelssohn* (London, Bentley, 1869; reprinted, New York, Vienna House, 1972).

M. E. von Glehn (ed.) *Goethe and Mendelssohn* (New York, Haskell, 1970).

Felix Moscheles, *The Letters of Mendelssohn* (New York, Books for Libraries Press, Reprint-1970).

Fanny Raymond Ritter (trans.) *Music and Musicians* (London: W. Reeves, 1877).

G. Selden-Goth (ed.). *Felix, Mendelssohn Letters* (New York: Kraus Reprint, 1969).

Lady Wallace (trans.) *Letters from Italy and Switzerland by Mendelssohn* (New York, Books for Libraries Press, Reprint, 1970)

Lady Wallace (trans.) *Letters of Felix Mendelssohn Bartholdy, from 1833 to 1847* (New York, Books for Libraries Press, Reprint, 1970).

Part I
Mendelssohn's Reflections on his own Music

Chapter One

Mendelssohn's General Outlook on Music

1830

In your last letter you seemed to be anxious lest, following my predilection for one of the great masters, I might devote myself too much to church music and be led into imitation. Such, however, is certainly not the case; for I believe that nowhere can one so swiftly outgrow the belief in the mere name as here, nor, on the other hand, feel a deeper reverence and esteem for what has been accomplished. What we know and revere is strange and unknown here; one almost admits that things must be that way. And then one finds immortal monuments which have come to light after centuries, without the possibility of discovering the names of their creators. So that nothing is valid except what has sprung from the deepest faith of the innermost soul. And though the aesthetes and scholars struggle to prove why this is beautiful and that less so, by means of purely external qualities like epochs, style, and whatever else their pigeon holes may be called, I believe that that is the only immutable criterion for architecture, painting, music, and everything else. If the object alone has not inspired creation, it will never speak from "heart to heart," and imitation is then nothing but the most superficial product of the most alien thoughts. Naturally, nobody can forbid me to enjoy the inheritance left by the great masters nor to continue to work at it, because not everybody has to begin at the beginning. But then it must be continued creation according to one's ability, and not a lifeless repetition of what is already there. And nowhere is it more wonderfully clear than in Rome that every genuinely personal and sincere work will find its appropriate place, however long it may take. And that is the thread to which I cling.[1]

1. Letter to Carl Zelter, Rome, December 18, 1830.

1831

And the more convinced I am that place, time, order, and the vast crowd of human beings awaiting, in the most profound silence, the moment for the music to begin, contribute largely to the effect.[2]

2. Letter to his Family, Rome, April 4, 1831.

In fact, as is the case with every masterpiece, I often suddenly and involuntarily think that the very same ideas might have occurred to me on a similar occasion.[3]

3. Letter to his Sisters, Naples, May 28, 1831.

For I require no underlying thought when I hear music—which to me is not "a mere medium to elevate the mind to piety" as they say here, but a distinct language which speaks clearly.[4]

4. Letter to Carl Zelter, Rome, June 31, 1831.

At first I resolved not to answer your letter until I had fulfilled your injunctions, and composed "Napoleon's Midnight Review"; and now I have to ask your forgiveness for not having done so, but there is a peculiarity in the matter. I take music in a very serious light, and I consider it quite inadmissible to compose anything that I do not thoroughly feel. It is just as if I were to utter a falsehood; for notes have as distinct a meaning as words, perhaps even a more definite sense. Now it appears to me almost impossible to compose for a descriptive poem. The mass of compositions of this nature do not militate against this opinion, but rather prove its truth; for I am not acquainted with one single work of the kind that has been successful. I could indeed have composed music for it in the same descriptive style, as Neukomm and Fischhof, in Vienna. I might have introduced a very novel rolling of drums in the bass, and blasts of trumpets in the treble, and have brought in all sorts of hobgoblins. But I love my serious elements of sound too well to do anything of the sort; for this kind of thing always appears to me a joke; somewhat like the paintings in juvenile spelling books, where the roofs are colored bright red, to make the children aware they are intended for roofs.[5]

5. Letter to Frau von Pereira, Genoa, July, 1831.

Recently, I was reading the episode of *Armida* in a carriage, surrounded by a company of Italian actors, who were incessantly singing Rossini's "*Ma trema, trema,*" when suddenly there recurred to my thoughts Gluck's "*Vous m'allez quitter,*" and I felt in a most melting mood. This is genuine music; thus have men felt, and thus have men spoken, and such strains can never die. I do cordially hate the present licentious style …

If I wish to hear Italian music, I must go to Paris or to England. The Germans however take it amiss when you say this, and persist *Par force* in singing, playing, and acquiring new ideas here, declaring this is the land of inspiration; while I maintain that inspiration is peculiar to no country, but floats about in the air.[6]

6. Letter to his Family, Milan, July 14, 1831.

A true musician, that is, one whose thoughts are absorbed in music, and not in money, or decorations, or ladies, or fame; it is doubly delightful when you find that, unaware, your own ideas exist and are being developed elsewhere …

The first and most indispensable quality of any artist is to feel respect for great men, and to bow down in spirit before them; to recognize their merits, and not to endeavor to extinguish their great flame, in order that his own feeble rushlight may burn a little brighter. If a person is incapable of feeling true greatness, I should like to know how he intends to make others feel it.[7]

7. Letter to Wilhelm Taubert, Lucerne, August 27, 1831.

Music composed for a purpose will never reach the heart, because it does not come from the heart.[8]

8. Letter to his Family, Wallenstadt, September 2, 1831.

None of the new libretti here would, in my opinion, be attended with any success if brought out for the first time on a German stage. One of the distinctive characteristics of all of them is precisely of a nature that I should resolutely oppose, although the taste of the present day may demand it, and I truly admit that it may, in general, be more prudent to go with the current than to struggle against it. I allude to that of immorality. This [libretto] produces effect, but I have no music for it. I consider it ignoble, and if the present epoch demands this style and considers it indispensable, then I will write oratorios.[9]

9. Letter to his Father, Paris, December 19, 1831.

1832

If I compose indifferent music, it will be quickly forgotten in Germany, but here [in Paris] it would be often performed and extolled, and sent to Germany, and given there on the authority of Paris, as we daily see. But I do not choose this; and if I am not capable of composing good music, I have no wish to be praised for it.[10]

10. Letter to Karl Immermann, Paris, February 21, 1832.

1833

Universality and everything bordering on aesthetics immediately render me dumb and dejected. Is it for me to tell you how you ought to feel? You strive to discriminate between an excess of sensibility and genuine good taste, and you say that a plant, too, may bloom itself to death. But there is no such thing as an excess of sensibility, and what is called a "too-much" is always rather a "too-little." The soaring, elevated emotions inspired by music —so welcome to the listeners—are no excess; let him, who is capable of emotions, feel them to the utmost of his capacity—and more so, if possible. If he dies of it, it will not be a death in sin, for nothing is certain but what is felt, or believed, or whatever term you may choose to employ. Moreover, the blooming of a plant never causes it to perish; except when the blooming is forced, and forced to the utmost. And such sickness is no more a blossom than sentimentality is sentiment.

It can only be deplored when anyone other than a genuine artist attempts to purify and restore the public taste. On such a subject words are only pernicious; deeds alone are effective. Even if people really feel this antipathy for the present, they can give nothing of themselves to replace it and therefore had better leave it alone. Palestrina effected a reform during his lifetime; he could not do so at the present time any more than Sebastian Bach or Luther.

The men are yet to come who will advance along the straight road—and it is they who will lead the others forward—or back to the ancient and correct path, which ought in fact to be termed the forward path; but they will write no books on the subject.[11]

11. Letter to Pastor Bauer, Berlin, March 4, 1833.

1834

A good performance makes one forget all the annoyances of stupidity and false notes.[12]

As a matter of sheer calculation the brass should be sparingly employed, let alone the question of Art! That's where I admire Handel's glorious style; when he brings up his timpani and trumpets towards the end, and thumps and batters about to his heart's content, as if he meant to knock you down—no mortal man can remain unmoved. I really believe it is far better to imitate such work, than to overstrain the nerves of your audience.[13]

1835

I cannot believe that impartial people can take pleasure in discords or be in any way interested in them: whether a few reporters puff the piece or not, matters little; their articles will leave no more traces than the composition. But what is the use of grumbling about bad music? Such things, however, make me feel the obligation of working hard and of exerting myself to put into shape to the best of my abilities that which I fancy to be music.[14]

Your search for flowers in the arid regions of modern composition makes me quite melancholy. It is so disheartening to see how colorless the heroes of our day are.[15]

1836

I have something else, too, on my conscience that I must tell you. Your *Overture* in D minor neither excited myself nor the musicians during its performance as I would have wished; it left us rather cold. This would have been of little consequence, but it was remarkable that all the musicians to whom I spoke said the same. The first theme and all the beginning, the melodies in A minor and A major, particularly delighted them; and their sympathy gradually subsided, till, when the close came, they had quite forgotten the striking impression of the theme, and no longer felt any interest in the music. This seems to me important, for I think it is connected with the difference which we have so repeatedly discussed together, and the want of

12. Letter to W. Horsley, Düsseldorf, April 3, 1834.

13. Letter to Ignaz and Charlotte Moscheles, Düsseldorf, June 26, 1834.

14. Letter to Ignaz Moscheles, Berlin, August 13, 1835.

15. Letter to Ignaz Moscheles, Leipzig, September 5, 1835.

interest with which you at all times regard your art, being now at length become perceptible to others. I would not say this to you, were it not that I am perfectly convinced of this being a point which must be left to each *individual*, as neither nature nor talents, even of the highest order, can remedy it; a man's own will alone can do so. Nothing is more repugnant to me than casting blame on the nature or genius of anyone; it only renders him irritable and bewildered, and does no good. No man can add one inch to his stature: in such a case all striving and toiling is vain, therefore it is best to be silent. Providence is answerable for this defect in his nature. But if it be the case, as it is with this work of yours, that precisely those very themes, and all that requires talent or genius (call it as you will), is excellent and beautiful and touching, but the development not so good,—then, I think, silence should not be observed; then, I think, blame can never be unwise, for this is the point where great progress can be made by the composer himself in his works. And as I believe that a man with fine capabilities has the absolute duty imposed on him of becoming something really superior, so I think that blame must be attributed to him if he does not develop himself according to the means with which he is endowed.

And I maintain that it is the same with a musical composition. Do not tell me that it is so, and therefore it must remain so. I know well that no musician can alter the thoughts and talents which Heaven has bestowed on him; but I also know that when Providence grants him superior ones, he *must also develop* them properly. Do not declare, either, that we were all mistaken, and that the execution was as much in fault as the composition. I do not believe it. I do believe that your talents are such that you are inferior to no musician, but I scarcely know one piece of yours that is systematically carried out.[16]

16. Letter to Ferdinand Hiller, Leipzig, January 24, 1836.

1837

I consider the publication of a work a serious matter for I maintain that no one should publish unless he is resolved to appear as an author for the rest of his life. For this purpose however a succession of works is indispensable. Nothing but annoyance can be expected from publishing where one or two works alone are in question ... or "manuscript for private circulation," which I also dislike.[17]

17. Letter to his Mother, Frankfurt, June 2, 1837.

1838

You wish me to give you an opinion about your compositions themselves; but you are well aware how superfluous I consider all such criticisms, whether of my own or of others; to go on working I consider the best and only thing to do, and when friends urge this after every fresh work, their doing so in itself contains a kind of verdict. I believe that no man ever yet succeeded in controlling and commanding the minds of others by *one work*; a succession of works all aiming at one point can alone do it. Such then is your function, and the duty which God has imposed on you by the talents he has given you.[18]

18. Letter to Edouard Franck, Leipzig, January 8, 1838.

I wish I could send you the wished for composition of the set of words you sent me; but it is altogether impossible for me to do anything in the way of prize composition; I cannot do it, if I would force myself to it; and when I was compelled to do so, when a boy, in competition with my sister and fellow-scholars, my works were always wonders of stupidity—not the tenth part of what I could do otherwise. I think that is the reason why I felt afterwards such an antipathy to prize-fighting in music, that I made a rule never to participate in it. Excuse me therefore, I should like to do as you wish me if I possibly could.[19]

19. Letter to Alfred Novello, Leipzig, April 7, 1838.

Would it not be well worth while for any publisher in Germany to publish just now some of Handel's principal oratorios from the *original scores*? This ought to be done by subscription, which would, I think, be successful, as not one of these scores exists with us. I thought of composing the organ parts for this purpose; they must, however, appear in small notes in the score, or in notes of another color, so that, first, those who wished it could have Handel pure; second, my organ parts in addition if required, and where there was no organ; and third, in a *supplement*, the organ part arranged for clarinets, bassoons, and other wind instruments of the modern orchestra, when no organ can be had.[20]

20. Letter to A. Simrock, Berlin, July 10, 1838.

In Beethoven and Handel and Bach one knows beforehand what is coming, and always must come, and a great deal more besides.[21]

21. Letter to Ferdinand Hiller, Berlin, July 15, 1838.

It is often grievous to me to see so many with the noblest aspirations but inferior talents, and others with great talents yet low tendencies; so that to see true genius combined with right good will is doubly cheering. People of the former class swarm here; almost all of the young musicians who visit me may, with few exceptions, be included in that number. They praise and prize Gluck and Handel, and all that is good, and talk about them perpetually and yet what they do is an utter failure, and so very tedious. Of the second class there are examples everywhere.[22]

22. Letter to Ferdinand David, Berlin, July 30, 1838.

On the occasion of a concert by Clara Novello all manner of artistic rivalries and petty bickering came to light, that would much better have remained in the dark. No, really, when these dear musicians begin to abuse one another, and to indulge in invective and backbiting, I could forswear all music, or rather all musicians. It does make me feel just like a cobbler; and yet it seems to be the fashion. I used to think it was only the way with the hacks of the profession; but the others are no better, and it takes a decent fellow with decent principles to resist the pernicious influence.[23]

23. Letter to Ignaz Moscheles, Leipzig, October 28, 1838.

1841

It is often very difficult, in fantastical airy subjects, to hit the right medium. If you grasp it too firmly, it is apt of become formal and prosaic; and if too delicately, it dissolves into air and melody, and does not become a defined form.[24]

24. Letter to "Herr X," Leipzig, January 22, 1841.

1842

It is a duty and an obligation, which one artist owes another, to help him as much as possible over difficulties and unpleasantnesses and to give him every assistance toward the fulfillment of his efforts, provided that they are honorable and the cause a good one ...

But just because the only consideration which ought reasonably to be entertained, with respect to publication, is that of intrinsic worth, and because it is the only one which ought to insure success if everything were carried on fairly in this world, and because it is too annoying to hear, forever repeated, the old story of the deserving and clever artists who at first experience the greatest difficulty in having their works brought out and become known, and who, afterward, are fussed over by everybody when one of their works happens to make a hit and gains the ear of the public (though, after all, neither the pleasure nor the fuss can make up for their former troubles), just because of all this I want you to act differently, and to put more belief in real work than chance success. Someone must put a stop to it some day, and the only question in such cases is how soon, and after how much unpleasantness. That is just the point at which a publisher may be of so much value and importance to an artist.[25]

25. Letter to N. Simrock, Frankfurt, September 21, 1842.

There is so much talk about music, and yet so little is said. For my part, I believe that words do not suffice for such a purpose, and if I found they did suffice I would finally have nothing more to do with music. People often complain that music is too ambiguous; that what they should think when they hear it is so unclear, where as everyone understands words. With me it is exactly the reverse, and not only with regard to an entire speech, but also with individual words. These, too, seem to be so ambiguous, so vague, so easily misunderstood in comparison to genuine music, which fills the soul with a thousand things better than words. The thoughts which are expressed to me by music that I love are not too indefinite to be put into words, but on the contrary, too definite. And so I find in every effort to express such thoughts, that something is right but at the same time, that something is lacking in all of them.[26]

26. Letter to Marc-Andre Souchay, Berlin, October 15, 1842.

Here, the outward aspect of things is now as much too flourishing as it formerly was too miserable for artists, which would be very pleasant for us, but it does harm to the cause. Art is becoming spoiled and sluggish, so we should rather be grateful to our present enemies than be angry with them.[27]

27. Letter to his Mother, Leipzig, December 11, 1842.

Chapter Two

Mendelssohn on his own Musical Studies

1826

Once more a thousand heartfelt thanks for the happy hours I owe to' your "Studies"; they will long find an echo in my mind.[1]

1. Letter to Ignaz Moscheles, Berlin, November 28, 1826.

1827

Thibaut does not know much about music, even his historical knowledge of it is limited, his judgments are mostly purely instinctive, I know more about it than he does, and yet I have learned a great deal from him and owe him many thanks. For he has shown me how to appreciate old Italian music, and warmed me with his passion. He showed me at once his large library of music of all nationalities and periods. He played and sang to me, explained the pieces, and several hours passed thus. We made music together and talked, and he lent me a magnificent piece of Lotti's to copy.[2]

2. Letter to his Mother, Heidelberg, September 20, 1827.

1831

I have music in my rooms at four o'clock in the afternoon, three times every week: Barmann, Breiting, Staudacher, young Poissl, and others, come regularly, and we have a musical picnic. In this way, I become acquainted with operas, which, most unpardonably, I have not yet either heard or seen; such as *Lodoiska, Faniska, Medea*; also the *Preciosa, Abu Hassan,* etc. The theatre lends us the scores.[3]

3. Letter to his Family, Munich, October 6, 1831.

Chapter Three

Mendelssohn on his Creative Process

1829
I had to be off into the country, found no carriage, and was obliged to walk in the cool of the evening; a number of musical ideas came to me, and I sang them out loud, for I was walking along a meadow path and met no one; the whole sky was grey with a purple streak on the horizon, and the thick cloud of smoke lay behind me. As soon as I find some peace and quiet, whether here or in Scotland, I shall write various things.[1]

Then I shall begin my *Reformation Symphony,* the *Scotch Symphony* and the *Hebrides* affair as well, which are also shaping themselves gradually. Besides this, I have a great deal of vocal music projected and in my head. Clementis sent me a few English verses and begged me to set them to music. This will be hard for me because I "must". [2]

1830
I am delighted to make so much music here in Munich, and though I have little time left to compose and to think, this gay life inspires me with many new ideas and proves to be cheering and refreshing.[3]

I cling to the ancient masters of painting, and study how they worked. Often, after doing so, I feel musically inspired, and since I came here I have been busily engaged in composition.[4]

I am healthier and happier than I have been for a long time, and take such delight in my work, and feel such an urge for it, that I expect to accomplish much more than I anticipated; indeed, I have already done a good deal. If it pleases Providence

1. Letter to his Family, London, June 7, 1829.

2. Letter to his Sisters, London, September 10, 1829.

3. Letter to Carl Zelter, Munich, June 22, 1830.

4. Letter to Carl Zelter, Venice, October 16, 1830.

to grant me a continuation of this happy mood, I look forward to the most delightful and productive winter.[5]

5. Letter to his Parents, Rome, November 8, 1830.

My favorite work that I am now studying is Goethe's *Lili's Park,* especially three portions: "*Kehr' ich mich um, und brumm,*" then "*Eh la menotte,*" and best of all, "*Die ganze Luft ist warm, ist blüthevoll,*" where decidedly clarinets must be introduced. I mean to make it the subject of a scherzo for a symphony.

A pianoforte concerto, too, that I wish to write for Paris, begins to float in my head.[6]

6. Letter to his Sister, Fanny, Rome, November 16, 1830.

1831

Since I left Vienna I have half composed Goethe's *First Walpurgis Night,* and have not courage to write it down.[7]

7. Letter to his Family, Rome, February 22, 1831.

If I could only compose one of my two symphonies! I must and will reserve the Italian one till I have seen Naples, which must play a part in it, but the other also seems to elude my grasp; the more I try to seize it, and the nearer the end of this delightful quiet Roman period approaches, the more am I perplexed, and the less do I seem to succeed.[8]

8. Letter to his Family, Rome, March 1, 1831.

The moment my work ceases to progress, I always hope to find some resource in the open air, so I go out but think of anything and everything except my work, and do nothing but wander about.[9]

9. Letter to his Family, Rome, March 29, 1831.

You reproach me that I am twenty-two and not yet famous. To this I can answer nothing; but if it had been the will of God that at twenty-two I should be famous, then famous I most likely should be. I cannot help it, for I compose as little with a view to becoming famous as of becoming a Kapellmeister. It would be delightful to be both, but as long as I am not positively starving, I look upon it as my duty to compose just how and what is written in my heart, and to leave the effect it will make to Him who takes heed of greater and better things. As time goes on I think more deeply and sincerely of that,—to write only as I feel, to have less regard than ever to outward results, and when I have produced a piece that has flowed from my heart—whether it is afterwards to bring me fame, honors, orders, or snuff-boxes, does not concern me.[10]

10. Letter to Eduard Devrient, Milan, July 13, 1831.

Every day I am more sincerely anxious to write exactly as I feel, and to have even less regard than ever for outside opinions; and when I have composed a piece just as it sprang from my heart, then I have done my duty; whether hereafter it brings fame, honor, decorations, or snuffboxes, etc., is a matter of indifference to me.[11]

11. Letter to Edward Devrient, Milan, July 15, 1831.

I can unfortunately form no judgment of my new compositions; I cannot tell whether they are good or bad; and this arises from the circumstance that all the people to whom I have played anything for the last twelve months, forthwith glibly declared it to be wonderfully beautiful, and that will never do. I really wish that some one would let me have a little rational blame once more, or what would be still more agreeable, a little rational praise, and then I should find it less indispensable to act the censor towards myself, and to be so distrustful of my own powers.[12]

12. Letter to his Family, Untersee, August 10, 1831.

The thing in which all my wishes would meet would be an opera; for I confess to you for the last six months I have had an incredible longing to set about one. I cannot think of instrumental music now, because I have nothing but voices and choruses buzzing around me, and I shall have no peace till I have worked it out. I must enter upon the new path that is in my thoughts, and make some way upon it before I can be sure whither it will lead me—and how soon. I already begin to feel sure, in instrumental music, what I ought to strive after, and because I have accomplished more in it and work with more certainty and clearness. In short, the spirit moves me.[13]

13. Letter to Eduard Devrient, Lucerne, August 27, 1831.

In the valley of Engelberg I found Schiller's "Wilhelm Tell," and on reading it over again, I was enchanted and fascinated anew by such a glorious work of art, and by all the passion, fire, and fervor it displays. An expression of Goethe's suddenly recurred to my mind. In the course of a long conversation about Schiller, he said that Schiller had been able to supply two great tragedies every year, besides other poems. This business-like term "supply" struck me as the more remarkable on reading this fresh, vigorous work; and such energy seemed to me so wonderfully grand that I felt as if, in the course of my life, I had not yet produced anything of importance; all my works seem so isolated. I feel as if I, too, must one day supply something. Pray do not think this presumptuous; but rather believe that I only say so because I know what ought to be, and what is not.[14]

14. Letter to Edward Devrient, Lucerne, August 27, 1831.

I shall never forget the time that I have just spent roaming about the mountains' [of Switzerland] on foot, all alone, without knowing a soul, and thinking of nothing but the new and wonderful things that burst upon me every moment.[15]

15. Letter to Goethe, Lucerne, August 28, 1831.

It is a glorious feeling to waken in the morning and to know that you are going to write the score of a grand allegro with all sorts of instruments, and various oboes and trumpets, whilst bright weather holds out the hope of a cheering, long walk in the afternoon.[16]

16. Letter to his Family, Munich, October 6, 1831.

1832

I receive numbers of commissions on all sides, and some so gratifying that I exceedingly regret not being able to accept them.[17]

17. Letter to his Father, London, June 1, 1832.

My life here begins slowly to take on a regular routine, but I still cannot get down to work. The morning and evening service for Novello which I have started does not count; that is just a daily chore—every morning one hour, and double canons to my heart's content—in other words, depending on my boredom. So I lie fallow and wait for better times, which, God willing, may come soon. I decided that your songs should get me into my stride again—when I begin to compose once more, I shall not stop again. And so I am awaiting them with twofold impatience; it would be nice if it turned out that they should be the first to set me going again.[18]

18. Letter to Karl Klingemann, Berlin, August 4, 1832.

I am working on the Morning Service for Novello, but it does not flow naturally; so far a lot of counterpoint and canons, and nothing more.[19]

19. Letter to Ignaz Moscheles, Berlin, August 10, 1832.

1833

Do not expect too much of the compositions I shall bring with me. You will be sure to find frequent traces of moodiness, which I can shake off only slowly and by dint of an effort. I often feel as if I had never composed at all, and had to learn everything over again; now, however, I have got into better trim, and my last things will sound better.[20]

Since at this moment a whole mass of music is buzzing in my head, I trust that it will not, please God, pass away quickly.[21]

You are probably aware that I directed the Music Festival in Düsseldorf and subsequently decided to take up my abode there for two or three years—nominally in order to direct church music and the Vocal Association, and probably also a new theater which is now being built—but in reality for the purpose of securing quiet and leisure for composition.[22]

1834

My own poverty in shaping new forms for the piano struck me again more forcibly while I was writing the *Rondo* [in E♭, Op. 29]. It is there that I got into difficulties and had to toil and labor, and I am afraid you will notice it. But how I am to start writing a calm and quiet piece (as you advised me last spring) I really do not know. All that passes through my head in the shape of piano music is about as calm and quiet as Cheapside; and when I sit down to the piano and compel myself to start improvising very quietly, it is of no use—by degrees I fall back into the old ways.

You can hardly imagine how much better and brighter I feel for the last two months' work, and how much more easily I get on with it. So I must keep it up and get into full swing. My birthday came just in time to remind me how necessary this was.[23]

My having composed beforehand the pieces bespoken by the Philharmonic and the English publishers, was owing not only to having received the commission, but also to my own inward impulse, because it is really very long since I have written—or worked at anything steadily, for which a certain mood is indispensable.[24]

20. Letter to Ignaz Moscheles, Berlin, February 27, 1833.

21. Letter to Pastor Bauer, Berlin, April 6, 1833.

22. Letter to Julius Schubring, Coblenz, September 6, 1833.

23. Letter to Ignaz Moscheles, Düsseldorf, February 7, 1834.

24. Letter to his Father, Düsseldorf, March 28, 1834.

1835

There are good days, and most enjoyable ones, when the work prospers, and I have a long morning to myself in my own quiet room; then life is charming indeed.[25]

It strongly revived my feeling as to the utter impossibility of my ever composing anything with a view to competing for a prize. I should never be able even to make a beginning.[26]

I do feel sometimes as if I should never succeed; and today I am quite dissatisfied with my work.[27]

One passage [of text] for *St. Paul,* was excellent, "*Der Du der recht Vater bist.*" A chorus for it came forthwith- into my head, which I shall very soon write down.[28]

I have an awful reverence for print, and I must go on improving my things until I feel sure they are all I can make them."[29]

1836

[Regarding *St. Paul*] In many points, especially as to subordinate matters in so large a work, I only succeed by degrees in realizing my thoughts and expressing them clearly; in the principal movements and melodies I can no longer indeed make any alteration, because they occur at once to my mind just as they are; but I am not sufficiently advanced to say this of *every* part. I have now, however, been working for rather more than two years at one oratorio; this is certainly a very long time, and I rejoice at the approach of the moment when I shall correct the proofs, and be done with it, and begin something else.[30]

How the oratorio went off you heard long ago. There was much that pleased me at the performance, and much that dissatisfied me; and even now I am at work on certain parts ... so much is there that completely fails to express my idea, in fact, does not even come near it. You have often advised me not to alter so much, and I am quite aware of the disadvantages of doing so; but if, on the one hand, I have been fortunate enough to express my idea in some parts of my work, and

---

25. Letter to Charlotte Moscheles, January 10, 1835.

26. Letter to Ludwig Spohr, Düsseldorf, March 8, 1835.

27. Letter to Ignaz Moscheles, Düsseldorf, March 25, 1835.

28. Letter to Julius Schubring, Leipzig, December 6, 1835.

29. Recalled by Eduard Devrient.

30. Letter to his Sister, Rebecca, Frankfurt, July 2, 1836.

have no desire to change those, I cannot help striving, on the other hand, to express my idea in other parts, and, if possible, throughout. But the task begins to weigh heavily upon me, as I am gradually more and more attracted by other work. I wish I could finish a few symphonies and that sort of thing in the course of the year.[31]

31. Letter to Ignaz Moscheles, Frankfurt, July 20, 1836.

The whole time I have been here I have worked at *St. Paul*, because I wish to publish it in as perfect a form as possible. In many points, especially subordinate ones in so large a work, I only succeed by degrees in realizing my thoughts more closely and in expressing them clearly; in the principal movements and melodies I can no longer make any alteration, because they occur suddenly to my mind just as they are; but I am not yet sufficiently advanced to say this of the whole.[32]

32. Letter to his Sister Rebecca, Frankfurt, August 2, 1836.

1837

I may well say that I now see, beyond doubt, that all [the attention] is only bestowed on me because in the course of my work I do not in the least concern myself as to what people wish and praise and pay for, but solely as to what I consider good, so I shall now less than ever allow myself to be turned aside from my own path.[33]

33. Letter to his Mother, Leipzig, October 4, 1837.

1838

You laugh, perhaps, and see me in the spirit as the true Philistine, with a cotton nightcap on my head, and going along with the usual snail's pace of my countrymen. Do not believe it; anyhow I give myself every trouble not to fall into the snail's pace, by working diligently and ceaselessly at such things as may, I hope, ensure me from it, and at the same time, I hope, save me from all that exaggeration and over-excitement, if it be possible in these days to escape from it.[34]

34. Letter to Madame Kiene, Leipzig, February 24, 1838.

This evening Madame Botgorscheck's concert takes place,—an excellent contralto singer, who persecuted me so much to play, that I agreed to do so, and it did not occur to me till afterwards that I had nothing either short or suitable to play, so I resolved to compose a rondo, not one single note of which was written the day before yesterday, but which I am to perform this evening with the whole orchestra, and rehearsed this morning. It sounds very gay; but how I shall play it the gods alone know,—indeed hardly they, for in one passage I have marked a pause of fifteen bars in the accompaniment, and have not as yet the most remote idea what I am to introduce during this time.[35]

35. Letter to his Family, Leipzig, April 2, 1838.

I have a symphony in my head which will soon be launched. In B-flat.[36]

36. Letter to Ferdinand Hiller, Berlin, July 15, 1838.

I feel that in every fresh piece I succeed better in learning to write exactly what is in my heart, and, after all, that is the only right rule I know.[37]

37. Letter to Ferdinand David, Berlin, July 30, 1838.

Where is it that you find beauty when I am working at a quartet or a symphony? Merely in that portion of myself that I transfer to it, or can succeed in expressing.[38]

38. Letter to Conrad Schleinitz, Berlin, August 1, 1838

Piano pieces are not the most enjoyable form of composition to me right now; I cannot even write them with real success; but I sometimes need a new piece to play, and if now and then something really suitable for the piano comes into my head, why should I be afraid of writing it down? Moreover, a very important branch of piano music, and one of which I am particularly fond—trios, quartets and other pieces with accompaniment, genuine chamber music—is quite forgotten now and I feel a great urge to do something new of this kind.[39]

39. Letter to Ferdinand Hiller, Berlin, August 17, 1838.

I had intended publishing several things at this time, instead of which here I am correcting parts, marking tempi, and attending to the long list of *odiosa* that are always sure to take a dire revenge on the man who dares neglect them.[40]

40. Letter to Ignaz Moscheles, Leipzig, October 28, 1838.

1839

I want to write a new concerto, but so far it is swimming about in my head in a shapeless condition. A new oratorio, too, I have begun; but how it is to end and what is to come in the middle heaven only knows.[41]

41. Letter to Ignaz Moscheles, Leipzig, November 30, 1839.

1841

Now for my critical spectacles, and a reply about your Becker "Rheinlied." I like it very much; it is well written, and sounds joyous and exhilarating, but (for a *but* must of course be uttered by every critic) the whole poem is quite unsuitable for composition, and essentially unmusical. I am well aware that in saying this I rashly throw down the gauntlet both to you, and many of my colleagues in Germany; but such is my opinion, and the worst part of it is, that I am confirmed in it by most of the compositions that I know. (For Heaven's sake, let this remain a secret between us, otherwise, as journalists publish every trifle nowadays, I may possibly be some day conveyed across the frontiers as a Frenchman.) But, jesting aside, I can only imagine music when I can realize the mood from which it emanates; mere artistically correct tones to suit the rhythm of the poetry, becoming *forte* when the words are vehement, and *piano* when they are meek, sounding very pretty, but expressing nothing,—I never yet could comprehend; and still such is the only music I can discover for this poem. Neither forcible, nor effective, nor poetical, but only supplementary, collateral, musical music. The latter, however, I do not choose to write. In such cases, the fable of the two vases often recurs to me, who set off together on a voyage, but in rolling to and fro one smashed his companion, the one being made of clay and the other of iron.[42]

42. Letter to Julius Schubring, Leipzig, February 27, 1841.

I perceive a certain spirit, especially in your overture, which I myself know only too well, for in my opinion it caused my *Reformation Symphony* to fail, but which can be surely and infallibly banished by assiduous work of different kinds. Just as the French, by conjuring tricks and overwrought sentiment, endeavor to make their style harrowing and exciting, so I believe it is possible, through a natural repugnance to this style, to fall into the other extreme, and so greatly to dread all that is *piquant* or sensuous, that at last the musical idea does not remain sufficiently bold or interesting; that instead of a tumour there is a wasting away …

The most important point is to make a theme, or anything of the kind which is in itself musical, really interesting …

As ideas cannot be either more highly finished or sharpened, but must be taken and made use of as they come, and as a kind Providence sends them.[43]

43. Letter to Julius Rietz, Leipzig, April 23, 1841.

1842

The question is then solely what is felt and experienced within a man's own breast, and uttered from the depths of his heart, be it grave or gay, bitter or sweet,—character and life are displayed here; and in order to prevent existence being dissipated and wasted when brilliant and happy, or depressed and destroyed when the reverse, there is but one safeguard,—to work, and to go on working. So, for your sake, I have only *one* wish, that you may bring to light what exists within you, in your nature and feelings, which none save yourself can know or possess. In your works, go deeper into your inmost being, and let them bear a distinct stamp; let criticism and intellect rule as much as you please in all outward questions and forms, but in all inner and original thought, the heart alone, and genuine feeling. So work daily, hourly, and unremittingly,—there you never can attain entire mastery or perfection; no man ever yet did, and therefore it is the highest vocation of life.[44]

44. Letter to Carl Eckert, Berlin, January 26, 1842.

1843

As long as the compositions remain here with me they never cease to torment me, because I so much dislike to see such nice, clean manuscript pass into the dirty hands of engravers, customers and the public, and I bolster up a little here, smooth out a little there and go on improving them just in order to keep them here. But when the proofs are once here, they are as foreign and indifferent to me as if they had been written by a stranger.[45]

45. Letter to Karl Klingemann, Leipzig, June 12, 1843.

Ever since I began to compose, I have remained true to my starting principle: not to write a page because no matter what public, or what pretty girl wanted it to be thus or thus; but to write solely as I myself thought best, and as it gave me pleasure.[46]

46. Letter to Eduard Devrient, Leipzig, June 28, 1843.

"He spoke disparagingly of ideas that had been waited for and contrived, and said that when one had at heart to compose music, the first involuntary thought would be the right one, even though it might not be so new or so striking, or though it might recall Sebastian Bach; if it did, it was a sign that so it was to have been."[47]

47. Recalled by Eduard Devrient.

1846

I have been back at work on *Elijah* with full vigor, and I hope to eliminate successfully many things that disturbed me at the first performance. Unfortunately I only discover these things *post festum*. I hope to be able to express what I wish more precisely, and I intend to review everything that does not suit me perfectly, with the greatest care.[48]

48. Letter to Karl Klingemann, Leipzig, December 6, 1846.

Mendelssohn's Search for an Opera Libretto

1831

You want me to devote myself to operas, and think it is wrong in me not to have done so long ago. I respond: give me a really good text, and in a few months it shall be composed; every day I long anew to write an opera. I know I could produce something bright and fresh, but I have no words. And a libretto that does not quite kindle my enthusiasm I am determined not to set. If you know any man capable of writing an opera, tell me his name for heaven's sake, I am only looking for him.[49]

49. Letter to Eduard Devrient, Milan, July 13, 1831.

I, for my part, feel at this moment the most urgent desire to write an opera, and yet I scarcely have the leisure to commence even any smaller work; but I do believe that if the libretto were to be given me today, the opera would be written by tomorrow, so strong is my impulse towards it. Formerly the bare idea of a symphony was so exciting, that I could think of nothing else when one was in my head; the sound of instruments has such a solemn and heavenly effect ... but there is nothing I so strongly covet as a real opera.[50]

50. Letter to Wilhelm Taubert, Lucerne, August 27, 1831.

I am sure I need not say that I will not compose music for any words I do not consider really good, and which do not inspire me. I shall reflect deeply on the poem before I begin the music.[51]

51. Letter to his Father, Paris, December 19, 1831.

1835

How gladly would I write an opera! but near and far I can find no libretto and no poet. Those who have the genius of poetry abhor music, or know nothing of the theater; others are neither acquainted with poetry, nor with mankind, only with the boards and lights and wings and canvas. Thus I never succeed in finding the opera which I have so eagerly, yet vainly striven to procure. I regret this more every day.[52]

52. Letter to Ludwig Spohr, Düsseldorf, March 8, 1835.

1836

I long to write an opera; but of that, I am afraid, there is not the least prospect. I am looking in vain throughout Germany and elsewhere for someone to help me realize this and other musical plans, and I despair of finding him. It is really absurd to think that in all Germany one should not be able to meet a man who knows the stage and writes tolerable verses; and yet I positively believe there is none to be found.[53]

53. Letter to Ignaz Moscheles, Frankfurt, July 20, 1836.

1840

Planche's text can never, even with the best will on both sides, become the kind of work I want; I am disposed to give up this attempt, too, as being utterly hopeless. I would rather never compose an opera at all, than one which I considered mediocre from the very start. Moreover, I could not possibly write such a work were you to give me the whole kingdom of Prussia ...

The scenario may be prolix or brief, detailed or merely sketched, on these points I do not presume to dictate, nor to decide whether the opera should be in three, four or five acts. If it is really good—just as it is written—then eight acts would not be too much for me, nor a single act too little. The same holds true as to whether or not there should be a ballet, the only criterion being whether or not it harmonizes with the musical and general feeling of the work.[54]

54. Letter to I. Fuerst, Leipzig, January 4, 1840.

Do you know that your suggestion as to the "Nibelungen" seems most interesting to me? It has been constantly in my head ever since, and I mean to spend my first day of leisure reading the poem, for I have forgotten the details and can only recall the outlines and the general coloring which seem to me gloriously dramatic.[55]

55. Letter to his Sister Fanny, Leipzig, November 14, 1840.

1843

I will then return you the opera libretto; much of it I like, above all the singable, throughout musical verses, also the subject of the love-spell, which in my thinking would give scope for a fine earnest composition. But, as a whole, the form of an opera in five acts, with spoken dialogue, is not congenial to me. I should not like to compose an opera with dialogue, which I would even prefer to see eliminated from shorter operas, but in an opera of five acts I should -consider continuous music essential.[56]

56. Letter to -Eduard Devrient, Leipzig, June 28, 1843.

1845

I feel as if it were a duty for me, too, to lend a hand to the cause of German opera, and record my vote in score; and it is a duty, although it does not depend on me to perform it. It appears that I do not possess the talent to arrange a plot into scenes; this is the one thing wanting; verses are easily to be procured, even I could write bad ones; this is no difficulty. Since I have been here I have daily employed my leisure hours in reading, and endeavored to contrive a plot, and put it into shape. The whole of Zschokke, all sorts of historical works, etc., I have plowed over with this intent but nothing comes of it; I have not the capacity for doing it.[57]

57. Letter to Eduard Devrient, Frankfurt, April 26, 1845.

Chapter Four

Mendelssohn on his own Compositions

Overture für Harmoniemusik, Op. 24 [1824]

1839

I wanted it published because I thought it would give some people pleasure, and because it is easy and there are parts in it I like.[1]

1. Letter to Ignaz Moscheles, Leipzig, January 13, 1839.

Three Fantasies for Pianoforte, Op. 16 [1829]

1829

I owe the Taylor girls three of my best piano compositions. When the two younger sisters saw that I took the carnations and rose in earnest and began to compose, the youngest once came with little, yellow, open bells in her hair, assuring me they were trumpets, and asking me whether I could not introduce them into the orchestra, as I had talked the other day of wanting new instruments; and when in the evening we danced to the miners' music and the trumpets were rather shrill, she gave it as her opinion that her trumpets would do better to dance to, so I wrote a dance for her—to which the yellow flower-bells played. For the middle one I composed "The Rivulet," which had pleased us so much during our ride that we dismounted and sat down beside it. This last piece, I believe, is the best of its kind that I have done; it is so slow-moving and quiet, and a little boringly simple, that I have played it to myself every day, and have got quite sentimental over it.[2]

2. Letter to his Sisters, London, September 10, 1829.

Songs without Words for Pianoforte, Op. 19 & 30 [1829]

1842

If you ask me what I was thinking of when I wrote it, I would say: just the song as it stands. And if I happen to have had certain words in mind for one or another of these songs, I would never want to tell them to anyone because the same words never mean the same things to different people. Only the song can say the same thing, can arouse the same feelings in one person as in another, a feeling which is not expressed, however, by the same words.[3]

3. Letter to Marc-Andre Souchay, Berlin, October 15, 1842.

The Herbrides Overture for Orchestra, Op. 26 [1830]

1830

I intend to finish my overture to the "Einsame Insel" as a present to you. You would probably say that you could not read my manuscript, but still I should have offered you the best it was in my power to give.[4]

4. Letter to his Father, Rome, December 10, 1830.

1832

I cannot bring out "The Hebrides" here, because ... I do not consider it finished; the middle movement forte in D major is very stupid, and the whole modulations savor more of counterpoint, than of train oil and seagulls and salt fish—and it ought to be exactly the reverse. I like the piece too well to allow it to be performed in an imperfect state, and I hope soon to be able to work at it, and to have it ready for England, and the Michaelmas fair at Leipzig.[5]

5. Letter to Karl Immermann, Paris, January 21, 1832.

Last Monday "The Hebrides" was given for the first time in the Philharmonic; it went admirably, and sounded very quaint among a variety of Rossini pieces. The audience received both me and my work with extreme kindness.[6]

6. Letter to his Father, England, May 18, 1832.

Small Church Forms

1830

Before I left Vienna, a friend of mine made me a present of Luther's Hymns, and on reading them over I was again so much struck by their power that I intend to compose music for several next winter. Since I have been here, I have nearly completed the chorale, *"Aus tiefer Noth"* and the Christmas hymn, *"Von Himmel hoch,"* is already in my Head ...

I finished two little pieces of sacred music in Vienna—a chorale in three movements for chorus and orchestra, *"O Haupt voll Blut und Wunden,"* and an *Ave Maria*.[7]

7. Letter to Carl Zelter, Venice, October 16, 1830.

1839

If in that performance of my Psalm at the Academy, they got into trouble with the Quintet it is lucky I was not there; for that is my favorite movement, and false notes make me savage.[8]

8. Letter to Ignaz Moscheles, Leipzig, February 27, 1839.

1841

As to the tempi in my Psalm, all I have to say is, that the passage of the Jordan must be kept very watery; it would have a good effect if the chorus were to reel to and for, that people might think they saw the waves; here we have achieved this effect.[9]

9. Letter to his Sister, Fanny, Leipzig, February 14, 1841.

Concerto for Pianoforte, Op. 25 [1830]

1833

Thank you very much for the letter you sent me from Lindblad [Music Director in Stockholm]. It gave me great pleasure, and made me like my concerto far better than I did before. That a piece so rapidly sketched as this pianoforte concerto should cause pleasure to so genuine a musician, enhances mine.[10]

10. Letter to his Father, Berlin, December 28, 1833.

Meerstille und glückliche Fahrt, for Orchestra, Op. 27 [1832]

1834

I must revise my *Meeresstille*, that is to say, rewrite nearly the whole of the Allegro.[11]

11. Letter to Eduard Devrient, February 5, 1834.

The Meeresstille I have entirely remodeled this winter, and think it is now some thirty times better.[12]

12. Letter to Pastor Schubring, Düsseldorf, August 6, 1834.

Die erste Walpurgnisnacht, Op. 60 [1832]

1831

Since I left Vienna I have half composed Goethe's "First Walpurgis Night," and have not courage to write it down. The composition has now taken shape, and become a grand cantata, with full orchestra, and may turn out quite amusing.[13]

13. Letter to his Family, Rome, February 22, 1831.

All I need now is a short overture; if that occurs to me, the thing is complete, and I can write it out in a couple of days. Then I shall leave all notes and their requisite music paper here, go off to Naples, where, please God, I mean to do nothing.[14]

14. Letter to his Family, Rome, March 29, 1831.

This whole letter seems to hover in uncertainty, or rather I do so in my *Walpurgis Night,* whether I am to introduce the big drum or not. *"Zacken, Gabeln, und wilde Klapperstücke,"* seem to force me to the big drum, but moderation dissuades me. At all events a vast noise is indispensable.[15]

15. Letter to his Family, Naples, April 27, 1831.

I have been writing a large composition that perhaps will one day make some effect, *"The first Walplurgis night"* of Goethe. I began it simply because it pleased me and excited me; I did not think of any performance. But now that it is finished, I see that it is well suited for a large concert piece.[16]

16. Letter to Eduard Devrient, Milan, July 13, 1831.

My week here has been one of the most agreeable and amusing that I have passed in Italy. In the first place, I immediately secured a small piano, and attacked with *rabbia* that endless *Walpurgis Night*, to finish the thing at last; and tomorrow morning it will be completed, except the overture; for as yet I have not quite made up my mind whether it shall be a grand symphony, or a short introduction breathing of spring. I must say the conclusion has turned out better than I myself expected. The hobgoblins and the bearded Druid, with- the trombones sounding behind him, diverted me immensely, and so I passed two forenoons very happily.[17]

17. Letter to his Family, Milan, July 14, 1831.

I have written a grand piece of music which will probably impress the public at large—the first "Walpurgnis Night" of Goethe. I began it simply because it pleased me, and inspired me, and gave no thought to its performance. But now that it lies finished before me, I see that it is quite suitable for a great *Concertstück*, and you must sing the bearded Pagan Priest. I wrote it expressly to suit your voice.[18]

18. Letter to Edward Devrient, Milan, July 15, 1831.

The *Walpurgis Nacht* is finished and revised, and the overture will soon be equally far advanced. The only person who has heard it as yet, is Mozart [the son], and he was so delighted with it that the well-known composition caused me fresh pleasure.[19]

19. Letter to his Family, Isola Bella, July 24, 1831.

I wrote you from Rome that I had been bold enough to compose your "First Walpurgis Night." I completed the work in Milan; it is a kind of cantata for chorus and orchestra, longer and more enlarged than I had planned it originally, because the more I was occupied with the task, the more important it seemed to me. Allow me to thank you for the heavenly words; when the old Druid offers up his sacrifice and the scene grows to immeasurable heights and solemnity, there is no need of inventing music; it is there already; everything sounds clear, and I started to sing the verses to myself before even thinking of the composition. The only thing I hope for, is that my music should be able to express how deeply I was moved myself by the beauty of the words.[20]

20. Letter to Goethe, Lucerne, August 28, 1831.

1842

I am really anxious at last to make the "Walpurgisnacht" into a symphony-cantata—for which it was originally intended, but did not become one from want of courage on my part.[21]

21. Letter to his Mother, Leipzig, November 28, 1842.

My *Walpurgis Nacht* is to appear once more in the second part, in a somewhat different garb indeed from the former one, which was somewhat too richly endowed with trombones, and rather poor in the vocal parts; but to effect this I have been obliged to rewrite the whole score from A to Z, and to add two new arias, not to mention the rest of the clipping and cutting. If I don't like it now, I solemnly vow to give it up for the rest of my life.[22]

22. Letter to his Mother, Leipzig, December 11, 1842.

1843

I have written the *Walpurgnisnacht* all over again from A to Z; in fact it is a different work now, and a hundred times better. But I am still in doubt about having it engraved.[23]

23. Letter to Ferdinand Hiller, Leipzig, March 3, 1843.

Te Deum [1832]

1832

I tried to begin the *Te Deum* in the style of your cathedral music, and it is now finished. Although it is not entirely as I wish it to be, and although I hope the following pieces will be better, I do not think it unworthy of being published.[24]

24. Letter to Vincent Novello, Berlin, August 22, 1832.

Symphony Nr. 5. ("Reformation") for Orchestra, Op. 107 [1832]

1830

Try to collect opinions as to the title I ought to select; *Reformation Symphony, Confession Symphony, Symphony for a Church Festival, Juvenile Symphony,* or whatever you like. Write to me about it, and instead of all the stupid suggestions, send me one clever one.[25]

25. Letter to his Sister, Weimar, May 25, 1830.

1841

I perceive a certain spirit, especially in your overture, which I myself know only too well, for in my opinion it caused my *"Reformation Symphony"* to fail, but which can be surely and infallibly banished by assiduous work of different kinds. Just as the French, by conjuring tricks and overwrought sentiment, endeavor to make their style harrowing and exciting, so I believe it is possible, through a natural repugnance to this style, to fall into the other extreme, and so greatly to dread all that is *piquant* or sensuous, that at last the musical idea does not remain sufficiently bold or interesting; that instead of a tumour there is a wasting away.[26]

26. Letter to Julius Rietz, Leipzig, April 23, 1841.

Symphony Nr. 4 ("Italian") for Orchestra, Op. 90 [1833]

1831

I have once more begun to compose with fresh vigor, and the Italian Symphony makes rapid progress; it will be the most amusing piece I have yet composed, especially the last movement. I have not yet decided on the adagio.[27]

27. Letter to his Family, Rome, February 22, 1831.

I must and will reserve the Italian symphony till I have seen Naples, which must play a part in it.[28]

28. Letter to his Family, Rome, March 1, 1831.

1833

I must now begin the last movement of my Italian Symphony; it gets into my fingers, spoils my letters, and takes up my time.[29]

29. Letter to Ignaz Moscheles, Berlin, February 27, 1833.

1834

The other day, Dr. Frank, whom you know, came to Düsseldorf, and I wished to show him something of my A major Symphony. Not having it here, I began writing out the Andante again, and in so doing I came across so many errata that I got interested and wrote out the Minuet and Finale too, but with many necessary alterations.

The first movement I have not written down, because, if once I begin with that, I am afraid I shall have to alter the entire subjects, beginning with the fourth bar,—and that means pretty nearly the whole first piece,—and I have no time for that just now. The dominant in the fourth bar strikes me as quite disagreeable; I think it should be the seventh (A-G).[30]

30. Letter to Ignaz and Charlotte Moscheles, Düsseldorf, June 26, 1834.

Die schöne Melusine Overture for Orchestra, Op. 32 [1833]

1833

I think that the overture to *Melusine* will be the best thing I have yet done.[31]

31. Letter to his Sister Rebecca, Düsseldorf, October 26, 1833.

1834

The "sf's" should be struck out everywhere as they really are quite wrong; it is not an abrupt accent that is intended, but a gradual swelling of the tone.[32]

32. Letter to Ignaz Moscheles, Düsseldorf, April, 1834.

I wrote this overture for an opera of Conradin Kreuzer's, which I saw this time last year in the Konigstadt Theater. The overture (I mean Kreuzer's) was encored, and I disliked it exceedingly, and the whole opera quite as much; but not Mlle Hahnel, who was very fascinating, especially in one scene, where she appeared as a mermaid combing her hair; this inspired me with the wish to write an overture which the people might not *encore*, but which would cause them more solid pleasure.[33]

33. Letter to his Sister, Fanny, Düsseldorf, April 7, 1834.

And so the people at the Philharmonic did not like my *Melusine*? Never mind; that won't kill me. I felt sorry when you told me, and at once played the overture through, to see if I too should dislike it; but it pleased me, and so there is no great harm done.[34]

34. Letter to Charolette Moscheles, Düsseldorf, May, 1834.

The great pleasure was my overture to *Melusina*, which was played in Leipzig for the first time, and pleased me extremely. In many pieces I know from the very beginning that they will sound well, and be characteristic, and so it was with this one as soon as the clarinet started off into the first bar. It was badly played; and yet I derived more pleasure from it than many a finished performance, and came home at night with a gladness of heart that I have not known for a long time.[35]

35. Letter to his Parents, Düsseldorf, August 4, 1834.

1836

Many persons here consider Melusina to be my best overture; at all events, it is the most deeply felt; but as to the fabulous nonsense of the musical papers, about red coral and green sea-monsters, and magic palaces, and deep seas, this is stupid stuff and fills me with amazement.[36]

36. Letter to his Sister, Fanny, Leipzig, January 30, 1836.

Fantasie for Pianoforte, Op. 28 [1833]

1834

I have ventured to dedicate to you ... a piece of which I am very fond.[37]

37. Letter to Ignaz Moscheles, Düsseldorf, February 7, 1834.

Oratorio, St. Paul, Op. 36 [1836]

1833

My work, which had given me many doubts recently, is finished; and now when I look it over, it gives me satisfaction, contrary to my expectation. I believe it is a good composition, and, be that as it may, I feel that it shows progress, and that is the main point.[38]

38. Letter to Pastor Bauer, Berlin, April 6, 1833.

1834

My Oratorio is making great progress. I am working at the second part, and have just written a Chorus in F sharp minor (a lively chorus of heathens) which I thoroughly relish myself.[39]

39. Letter to Ignaz and Charlotte Moscheles, Düsseldorf, June 26, 1834.

Last autumn, when I first established myself here, I got your letter with the notices for St. Paul; they were the best contributions I had yet received and that very same forenoon I began to ponder seriously on the matter, took up my Bible in the midst of all the disorder of my room, and was soon so absorbed in it that I could scarcely force myself to attend to other works which I was absolutely obliged to finish. I really did commence in spring, so many anxieties about my composition ensued, that they unsettled me. More than half of the first part is ready, and I hope to finish it in autumn, and the whole in February.[40]

40. Letter to Pastor Julius Schubring, Düsseldorf, July 15, 1834.

My Oratorio is not yet so advanced as you think it, for I have not quite finished the first part, which is to be shorter than the second; but if I proceed slowly it is at least without trombones, and I flatter myself to have been as moderate in the use of brass, as any enemy of the Birmingham industry or a friend to invalid trumpeters could have wished; for out of twelve Choruses in the first part, there are but two with the brass band, and the beginning Chorus is even without trumpets! Are you not satisfied with this? And am I not likely to become a writer whose dreams may be undisturbed by the ghosts of drummers and trumpeters arising and showing their wounds and crying, Remember how we got them! At least I am firmly convinced that if the idea of the thing lacks power all the trombones of Great Britain and Ireland are not able to supply it, and serve only to make the weakness of the idea more conspicuous.[41]

41. Letter to W. Horsley, Düsseldorf, August 23, 1834.

I have the second part now nearly all in my head, up to the passage where they take Paul for Jupiter, and wish to offer sacrifices to him, for which some five choruses must be found; but as yet I have not the faintest conception what—it is difficult.[42]

42. Letter to his Mother, Düsseldorf, November 4, 1834.

1835

I began an oratorio about a year ago, which I expect to finish next month, the subject of which is *St. Paul*. If the music only proves to be as good as I wish! At all events, I have enjoyed the most intense delight while engaged in writing it.[43]

43. Letter to Ludwig Spohr, Düsseldorf, March 8, 1835.

Today I am quite dissatisfied with my work, and should just like to write my Oratorio over again from beginning to end.[44]

One passage for *St. Paul,* was excellent, *"Du der rechte Vater bist."* A chorus for it came forthwith into my head, which I shall very soon write down. I shall now work with doubled zeal at the completion of St. Paul, for my father urged me to it in the very last letter he wrote to me, and he looked forward very impatiently to the completion of my work. I feel as if I must exert all my energies to finish it and to make it as good as possible.[45]

1836

During the whole of the rehearsals and the performance I thought little enough about directing, but listened eagerly to the general effect, and whether it went right according to my idea, without thinking of anything else. Many parts caused me much pleasure, others not so; but I learnt a lesson from it all, and hope to succeed better the next time I write an oratorio.[46]

How the oratorio went off you heard long ago. There was much that pleased me at the performance, and much that dissatisfied me; and even now I am at work on certain parts of the piano arrangement —which is to appear shortly—and on the orchestral score; so much is there that completely fails to express my idea, in fact, does not even come near it. You have often advised me not to alter so much, and I am quite aware of the disadvantages of doing so; but if, on the one hand, I have been fortunate enough to express my idea in some parts of my work, and have no desire to change those, I cannot help striving, on the other hand, to express my idea in other parts, and, if possible, throughout. But the task begins to weigh heavily upon me.[47]

The whole time I have been here I have worked at *St. Paul,* because I wish to publish it in as perfect a form as possible; and moreover, I am quite convinced that the beginning of the first and the end of the second part are now newly three times as good as they were —thus it was my duty. In many points, especially subordinate ones in so large a work, I only

44. Letter to Ignaz Moscheles, Berlin, August 13, 1835.

45. Letter to Julius Schubring, Leipzig, December 6, 1835.

46. Letter to Conrad Schleinitz, Köln, July 5, 1836.

47. Letter to Ignaz Moscheles, Frankfurt, July 20, 1836.

succeed by degrees in realizing my thoughts more closely and in expressing them clearly; in the principal movements and melodies I can no longer make any alteration, because they occur suddenly to my mind just as they are; but I am not yet sufficiently advanced to say this of the whole. I have now, however, been working for rather more than two years at this one oratorio; it is certainly a very long time.[48]

48. Letter to his Sister Rebecca, Frankfurt, August 2, 1836.

1837

Even with the orchestra, there are only a few numbers which quite satisfy me, and express exactly what I wished to convey. I intend soon to compose another, in which I hope to succeed better.[49]

49. Letter to Eduard Devrient, Frankfurt, May 15, 1837.

1839

The number of friends that *St. Paul* has gained me is really quite remarkable. I could never have anticipated it. It was performed twice in Vienna in the spring, and they want to have a festival there in November, with one thousand performers (*St. Paul* is to be given), which I shall probably go to conduct. This has surprised me the more, because no other work of mine has ever made its way into Vienna.[50]

50. Letter to Karl Klingemann, Hochheim, August 1, 1839.

Serenade and Allegro for Pianoforte and Orchestra, Op. 43 [1838]

1838

This evening Madame Botgorscheck's concert takes place,—an excellent contralto singer, who persecuted me so much to play, that I agreed to do so, and it did not occur to me till afterwards that I had nothing either short or suitable to play, so I resolved to compose a rondo, not one single note of which was written the day before yesterday, but which I am to perform this evening with the whole orchestra, and rehearsed this morning. It sounds very gay; but how I shall play it the gods alone know,— indeed hardly they, for in one passage I have marked a pause of fifteen bars in the accompaniment, and have not as yet the most remote idea what I am to introduce during this time.[51]

51. Letter to his Family, Leipzig, April 2, 1838.

String Quartet in D, Op. 44 [1838]

1838

I have just finished my third quartet in D major, and like it much. May it only please you as well!—I almost think it will, for it is more spirited, and seems to me likely to be more grateful to the players than the others.[52]

My third violin quartet in D major is finished; I like the first movement immensely ... especially a forte passage at the end.[53]

Ruy Blas Overture for Orchestra, Op. 95 1839]

1839

You wished to know how the overture to *Ruy Blas* went off. Famously. Six or eight weeks since an application was made to me in favor of a representation to be given for the Theatrical Pension Fund (an excellent benevolent institution here, for the benefit of which *Ruy Blas* was to be given). I was requested to compose an overture for it, and the music of the romance in the piece, for. It was thought the receipts would be better if my name appeared in the bills. I read the piece, which is detestable, and more utterly beneath contempt than you could believe, and said that I had no leisure to write the overture, but I composed the romance for them. The performance was to take place last Monday week; on the previous Tuesday the people came to thank me politely for the romance, and said it was such a pity I had not also written an overture, but they were perfectly aware that time was indispensable for such a work, and the ensuing year, if I would permit them, they would give me longer previous notice. This put me on my mettle. I reflected on the matter the same evening, and began my score. On Wednesday there was a concert rehearsal, which occupied the whole forenoon. Thursday the concert itself, yet the overture was in the hands of the copyist early on Friday; played three times in the theater, and given in the evening as an introduction to the odious play. Few of my works have caused me more amusing excitement.[54]

---

52. Letter to Ferdinand David, Berlin, July 30, 1838.

53. Letter to Ferdinand Hiller, Berlin, August 17, 1838.

54. Letter to his Mother, Leipzig, March 18, 1839.

Antigone, Op. 55 [1841]

1841

I have composed music for it to my heart's content. The subject in itself was glorious, and I worked at it with heartfelt pleasure.[55]

55. Letter to Ferdinand David, Berlin, October 21, 1841.

Symphony Nr. 3 ("Scottish") for Orchestra, Op. 56 [1842]

1831

The *Scotch Symphony* alone a not yet quite to my liking; if any brilliant idea occurs to me, I will seize it at once, quickly write it down, and finish it fast.[56]

56. Letter to his Family, Rome, February 22, 1831.

The finest season of the year in Italy is from the 15th of April to the 15th of May. Who can wonder that I find it impossible to return to my Scotish, misty mood? I have therefore had to lay aside the Scotch Symphony for the present.[57]

57. Letter to his Family, Rome, March 29, 1831.

Violin Concerto, Op. 64 [1844]

1838

I should also like to write a violin concerto for you next winter. One in E minor runs in my head, the beginning of which gives me no peace.[58]

58. Letter to Ferdinand David, Berlin, July 30, 1838.

Athalie Overture for Orchestra, Op. 74 [1845]

1840

In the midst of all this the composition of the overture to *Athalia,* which, being excessively troublesome, was no slight task.[59]

59. Letter to his Brother, Paul, Soden, July 17, 1844.

Oratorio, *Elijah*, Op. 70 [1846]

1838

I ought to have previously told you that the sheets you took away with you are by no means to be regarded as containing a mature design, but as a mere combination of the materials I had before me for the purpose of eventually forming a plan ...

I am anxious to do justice to the *dramatic* element, and, as you say, no epic narrative must be introduced.[60]

60. Letter to Pastor Schubring, Leipzig, November 1, 1838.

Thank you for the manuscripts you have from time to time sent me for *Elijah*; they are of the greatest possible use, to me, and though I may here and there make some alterations, still the whole affair by your aid, is now placed on a much firmer footing . With regard to the dramatic element, there still seems to be a diversity of opinion between us. In such a character as that of Elijah, like everyone in the Old Testament, except perhaps Moses, it appears to me that the dramatic should predominate,—the personages should be introduced as acting and speaking with fervor; not, however, for Heaven's sake, to become mere musical pictures, but inhabitants of a positive, practical world, such as we see in every chapter of the Old Testament; and the contemplative and pathetic element which you desire must be entirely conveyed to our apprehension by the words and the mood of the acting personages.[61]

61. Letter to Pastor Schubring, Leipzig, December 6, 1838.

1846

Once more I must trouble you about *Elijah*; I hope it is for the last time, and I also hope that you will at some future day derive enjoyment from it; and how glad I should be were this to be the case! I have now quite finished the first part, and six or eight numbers of the second are already written down. In various places, however, of the second part I require a choice of really fine Scriptural passages, and I do beg of you to send them to me!

The second part begins with the words of the queen, "So let the gods do to me, and more also," etc. (I Kings xix.2); and the next words about which I feel secure are those in the scene in the wilderness (same chapter, fourth and following verses); but between these I want, *first,* something more particularly characteristic of the persecution of the prophet; for example, I should like to have a couple of choruses *against* him, to describe the people in their fickleness and their rising in opposition to him; *secondly,* a representation of the third verse of the same passage; for instance, a duet with the boy, who might use the words of Ruth, "Where thou goest, I will go," etc. But what is Elijah to say before and after this? and what could the chorus say? Can you furnish me with, first, a duet, and then a chorus in this sense?

Then, till verse 15, all is in order; but there a passage is wanted for Elijah, something to this effect:—"Lord, as Thou willest, be it with me" (this is not in the Bible, I believe?) I also wish that *after* the manifestation of the Lord he should announce his entire submission, and after all this persecution declare himself to be entirely resigned, and eager to do his duty.

I am in need, too, of some words for him to say at, or before, or even after his ascension, and also some for the chorus. The chorus sings the ascension historically with

the words from II Kings ii.11, but then there ought to be a couple of very solemn choruses. "God is gone up" will not do, for it was not the Lord, but Elijah who went up; however, something of *that* sort. I should like also to hear Elijah's voice once more at the close.[62]

62. Letter to Julius Schubring, Leipzig, May 23, 1846.

During the whole hour and a half that it lasted, the big hall with its two thousand people and the large orchestra were all so concentrated on the subject in question, that not the slightest sound could be heard from the audience, and I was able to sway at will the enormous mass of orchestra and choir and organ.

No less than four choruses and four arias were encored, and in the whole first movement there was not a single mistake. Later there were several in the second half, but even these were unimportant. A young English tenor sang the last aria so beautifully that I was obliged to exercise great self-control in order not to be affected, and to beat time steadily.[63]

63. Letter to his Brother, on the first performance, Birmingham, August 26, 1846

Part II
Mendelssohn's View of the World of Music

Chapter Five

Mendelssohn's Observations on Performance and Performers

1829

M. Fetis has, it appears, thought fit to drag my name before the public by referring to some expressions which may have fallen from me in private conversation with him. While denying the right of M. Fetis thus to quote any private and detached expressions of mine in order to support his own opinions, I must, at the same time, question the justice of your holding me up to the British public as a co-censor with that gentleman. Whatever were the words used by me on the occasion referred to, they were uttered merely to give expression to a momentary feeling, caused by a performance, which, to use your own language, was "timid and unsatisfactory." Generally speaking, a single performance will, in no case, enable anyone to give a public judgment on the merits of an eminent composer.[1]

1. Letter to the Editor of Britannia, regarding a performance of Henry Purcell's *Te Deum*, London, July 8, 1829.

1833

Afterwards came a procession, playing my solemn march in E♭, the bass performers repeating the first part, while those in the treble went straight on; but this was of no consequence in the open air; and when I encountered them later in the day, they had played the march over so often that it went famously.

Previous to that Sunday, however, there was rather a touching scene. I must tell you that no really appropriate epithet exists for the music which has hitherto been given here. The chaplain came and complained to me of his dilemma; the Mayor had said that though his predecessor was evangelical and perfectly satisfied with the music, he himself intended to form part of the procession, and insisted that the music should be of a better class. A very peevish old musician, in a threadbare coat, was summoned. Hitherto it had been his office to beat time. When he came and they attacked him, he declared that he neither could or would have better music; that if we wanted to have it, we should look for somebody else; that he knew perfectly well what vast pretensions some people had nowadays; everything was expected to sound so beautiful; this had not been the case in his day, and he played just as well now as formerly. I was really very reluctant to take the affair out of his hands, though there could be no doubt that others would do infinitely better; and I could not help thinking how I should feel myself were I to be summoned some fifty years hence to a town hall, and have to speak in this way, and a young green-horn snubbed me, and my coat was shabby, and I had not the remotest idea why the music should sound better—and I felt rather uncomfortable.[2]

2. Letter to his Sister Rebecca, Düsseldorf, October 26, 1833.

1838

At the Singakademie a piece of my own was sung in such a manner that I should have got seriously angry if Cecile had not sat beside me and kept on saying: "Dear husband, do be calm!" They also played me some quartets and invariably bungled the very same passages that they had bungled ten years ago, and which made me furious ten years ago—another proof of the immortality of the soul.[3]

3. Letter to Ferdinand Hiller, Berlin, August 17, 1838.

On Pianoforte Playing

1832

The publishers [of Paris] are standing on each side of me like veritable Satans, demanding music for the piano, and offering to pay for it. By Heavens! I don't know whether I shall be able to withstand this, or write some kind of trio; for I hope you believe me to be superior to the temptation of a pot-pourri.[4]

4. Letter to Karl Immermann, Paris, January 21, 1832.

The sense for serious music is certainly not outstandingly well developed in Frankfort, and yet it is astonishing how well young lady amateurs play the *Wohltemperiertes Clavier*, the *Inventions* and all of Beethoven. They know everything by heart, they check every false note, and they possess a genuine musical culture.[5]

5. Letter to Carl Zelter, Paris, February 15, 1832.

1833

Why should I be forced to listen for the thirtieth time to all sorts of variations by Herz? They cause me less pleasure than rope-dancers or acrobats. In their case we have at least the barbarous excitement of fearing that they may break their necks, and of seeing that nevertheless they escape doing so. But those who perform feats of agility on the piano do not even endanger their lives, but only our ears. In such I take no interest. I wish I could escape the annoyance of being obliged to hear that the public demands this style; I also form one of the public, and I demand the exact reverse. Moreover, she played in the theatre between the acts, and that I consider most obnoxious. First, up goes the curtain, and I see before me India, with her pariahs and palm-trees and prickly plants, and then come death and murder, so I must weep bitterly; then up goes the curtain again, and I see Madame B __ with her piano, and a concert ensues in every variety of minor key, and I must applaud with all my might; then follows the farce of *"Ein Stündchen vor dem Potsdamer Thor,"* and I am expected to laugh. No! This I cannot stand.[6]

The other day I heard a Berlin pianist play the worst variations on the "God Save the King" that I have ever listened to, and that is speaking volumes. The man had great technical ability and good fingers; and yet his performance was hollow and lifeless.[7]

1834

Have you heard of a Mademoiselle Meyer who has gone with her father from here to London to play the piano? She must, some time or other, pass in review before Moscheles, and I should like above all things to hear of her doings in London. The father *would* set me up here as his daughter's rival, and, finding that I took no notice, is going to try what he can do in London.[8]

If Herz will only abstain from writing Variations for four hands, or, if that is too much to ask, if he will only avoid winding up with those Rondos that are so frightfully vulgar that I am ashamed to play them to decent people, then, for

6. Letter to Ignaz Moscheles, Berlin, 1833.

7. Letter to Ignaz Moscheles, Berlin, March 17, 1833.

8. Letter to Charlotte and Ignaz Moscheles, Düsseldorf, May 11, 1834.

aught I care, let him be made King of the Belgians. After all, I like him, he certainly is a characteristic figure of these time, of the year 1834; and as Art should be a mirror reflecting the character of the times,—as Hegel or some one else probably says somewhere,—he certainly does reflect most truly all salons and vanities, and a little yearning, and a deal of yawning, and kid gloves, and musk, a scent I abhor.[9]

9. Letter to Ignaz and Charlotte Moscheles, Düsseldorf, June 24, 1834.

1837

For really the piano music of the present day is such that I cannot make up my mind to play it through more than once; it is so desperately empty and poor that I usually get tired of it on the first page.[10]

10. Letter to Ignaz Moscheles, Speier, April 6, 1837.

The new pianoforte school can execute a few variations and *tours de force* cleverly enough, but all this facility, and coquetting with facility, no longer succeeds in dazzling even the public. There must be soul, in order to carry others along with you.[11]

11. Letter to his Mother, Bingen, July 13, 1837.

1843

You must not compare my playing with my music; I feel quite embarrassed by such an idea, and I am certainly not the man to prevent people worshipping the golden calf, as it is called in the fashion of the day. Moreover, I believe that this mode will soon pass away, even without opposition. True, a new one will certainly start up; on this account therefore it seems to me best to pursue one's own path steadily, and especially to guard against an evil custom of the day, which is not included in those you name, but which, however, does infinite harm,—squandering and frittering away talents for the sake of outward show. This is a reproach which I might make to most of our present artists, and to myself also more than I could wish.[12]

12. Letter to G. Otten, Leipzig, July 7, 1843.

On Singing

1829

Donzelli (Otello), full of bravura and flourishes fraught with meaning, shouts and forces his voice dreadfully, almost constantly singing a little too high, but with no end of *haut gout*.

In the last passionate scene where Malibran screams and raves almost disagreeably. Mme Malibran is a young woman, beautiful and splendidly made, bewigged, full of fire and power, and at the same time coquettish; setting off her performance partly with very clever embellishments of her own invention, partly with imitations of Pasta (it seemed very strange to see her take the harp and sing the whole scene exactly like Pasta). She acts beautifully, her attitudes are good, only it is unfortunate that she should so often exaggerate and so often border on the ridiculous and disagreeable.[13]

About the English style of singing I will say nothing, but will give you a specimen in December; you will fall from your chair with laughing. Neither do I like the Italian singers; the much renowned Donzelli is always singing sharp and roars fearfully; on the other hand, Malibran is above all praise. There are voices whose simple sound moves one to tears; she has such a one, and sings withal earnestly, passionately, and tenderly, and she acts well too. You should see her! That confounded Veluti is just passing beneath the window; he is a poor wretched creature, whose singing so excited my loathing that it pursued me into my dreams that night.[14]

The other night I heard Don Giovanni given by the Italians; it was funny. Pellegrini sang Leporello, and acted like an ape; at the end of his first song he introduced a string of cadences out of any half dozen Rossinian operas.[15]

1830

Schechner is very much gone off; the quality of her voice has become husky; she repeatedly sang flat, yet there were moments when her expression was so touching, that I wept in my own fashion.[16]

13. Letter to his Father, London, April 25, 1829.

14. Letter to Eduard Devrient, London, May 19, 1829.

15. Letter to Eduard Devrient, London, June 19, 1829.

16. Letter to his Family, Munich, June 6, 1830.

The Papal Choir's full complement is thirty-two, but they are said to be rarely complete. The conductor sings with them, and conducts with his voice by helping out in each part, when necessary jumping from a deep bass to a discant entrance in falsetto voice. There are no boys' voices and so far have never been any, and Baini, who complained that every year fewer sopranos become available, was almost offended when I asked if he could not substitute boys. As to the special style of performing Palestrina's music, which people say has been preserved by tradition in the Papal Chapel, I have been able to detect very little of it. It seemed to me that the only peculiarity in their way of singing consisted of forcing their voices almost throughout and holding the long notes in uniform and undiminished volume, which with us I think would be considered incorrect. But it sounds very good coming from the large, beautiful voices of the basses and sometimes from the tenors, too; only the top voices sometimes sound repulsively shrill.

It might also be reckoned among their oddities that they retain the little ornaments and trills such as were popular at the beginning of the last century, although that could really be called practically a mistake, because all the inner voices, without exception, participate in these embellishments and thus occasionally produce very strange sound effects ... [Here Mendelssohn gives several examples of improvisation in the Baroque style] You can imagine what a singular effect it has when it is sung consistently by all the inner voices through a whole Mass. Incidentally this style of [turning half-notes into dotted quarter-notes followed by an eighth-note which becomes an anticipation of the following pitch] is at times completely justified, and gives the whole thing a beautiful, smooth tone; and if now and then very peculiar dissonances result, the effect in the music they sing is not at all bad; but they had better not do it with Johann Sebastian Bach.

Their enunciation is so vague that it is hard to tell what words they are singing or whether they are singing any at all.

The precentors follow one another, each starting in a different key ... It makes a very strange impression; one entirely loses a sense of key and follows the notes without any guide, up and down, to the point where the first chord -of a piece broadens again, completely resolves the sense of uncertainty and gives back the feeling of the music.[17]

17. Letter to Carl Zelter, Rome, December 1, 1830.

I have listened daily to the Papal Choir. There again it struck me particularly how extraordinary everything is here. They did not sing particularly well, the compositions were poor, the congregation was not devout, and yet the whole effect was heavenly. This was only due to the fact that they were singing in the central nave of St. Peter's; the sounds are reflected from above and from every corner, they mingle, die away, and produce the most wonderful music. One chord melts into the other, and what no musician would dare, St. Peter's Church achieves.[18]

18. Letter to Carl Zelter, Rome, December 18, 1830.

1831

Be discreet and indulgent, and avoid fatiguing either yourself or the voices of your singers. Do not be irritable when things go badly; say very little on the subject to anyone. Lastly, above all, endeavor to prevent the choir feeling any tedium, for this is the principal point.[19]

19. Letter to his Sister, Fanny, on conducting. Rome, February 22, 1831.

The singers are the worst Italian ones I ever heard anywhere (except, indeed, in Italy), and those who wish to have a true idea of Italian singing must go to Paris or to London.[20]

20. Letter to his Family, Naples, May 17, 1831.

If you suppose that there are any Italian singers in Italy, you are profoundly in error. The prima donna in Rome is a native of Berlin. O misery! she sang execrably, and gave herself as many airs as a horse with bells. Could you but hear one of these Italian taught singers, what a total absence of all method they have; how much better and more purely a Bavarian barmaid sings than they; how they ape the little originalities, naughtinesses, and exaggerations of the great singers, and call *that* method.[21]

21. Letter to Eduard Devrient, Milan, July 13, 1831.

I hurried off to the Theatre Français, where Mars was to appear for the first time for a year past; (she is fascinating beyond conception; a voice that we shall never hear equaled causing you to weep, and yet to feel pleasure in doing so).[22]

22. Letter to his Sister, Fanny, Paris, December 28, 1831.

1832

The St. Cecilia Society alone would make it worth while to be in Frankfurt. The singers work with such enthusiasm and precision that it is a sheer delight to listen to them. It meets once a week and has two hundred members.[23]

23. Letter to Carl Zelter, Paris, February 15, 1832.

1840

Last night, at the twenty-fifth anniversary of the Liedertafel, I was as angry as if I had been a young boy. They sang so false, and talked even more falsely; and when it became peculiarly tiresome, it was in the name of "our German Fatherland," or "in the good old German fashion."[24]

24. Letter to his Sister, Fanny, Leipzig, October 24, 1840.

1841

I lately heard Pasta in *Semiramide*. She sings now so fearfully out of tune, especially in the middle notes, that it is quite painful to listen to her; but, of course, the splendid remains of her great talent, the traces of a first-class singer, are often unmistakable.[25]

25. Letter to President Verkenius, Berlin, August 23, 1841.

1846

The rich, full sounds of the orchestra and the huge organ, combined with the powerful choruses who sang with honest enthusiasm, the wonderful resonance in the grand giant hall, an admirable English tenor singer; Staudigl, too, who took all possible pains, and whose talents and powers you already well know, and in addition a couple of excellent second soprano and contralto solo singers; all executing the music with peculiar spirit, and the utmost fire and sympathy, doing justice not only to the loudest passages, but also to the softest *pianos*, in a manner which I never before heard from such masses, and, in addition, an impressionable, kindly, hushed, and enthusiastic audience,—all this is indeed sufficient good fortune for a first performance. In fact, I never in my life heard a better, or I may say so good a one, and I almost doubt whether I shall ever again hear one equal to it, because there were so many favorable combinations on this occasion. Along, however, with so much light, as I before said, there were also shadows, and the worst was the soprano part. It was all so neat, so pretty, so elegant, so slovenly, so devoid both of soul and head, that the music almost drives me mad when I think of it. The voice of the contralto, too, was not powerful enough to fill the hall ...

At least to *me, nothing* is so repugnant in music as a certain cold, soulless coquetry, which is in itself so unmusical, and yet so often adopted as the basis of singing, and playing, and music of all kinds. It is singular that I find this to be the case much less even with Italians than with us Germans. It seems to me that our countrymen must either love music in all sincerity, or they display an odious, stupid, and affected coldness, while an Italian throat sings just as it comes, in a straightforward way, though perhaps for the sake of money, but still not for sake of money, *and* aesthetics, *and* criticism, *and* self-esteem, *and* the right school, and twenty-seven thousand other reasons, none of which really harmonize with their real nature. [26]

26. Letter to Frau Frege, on the first performance of his "Elijah," in London, London, August 31, 1846.

On Opera

1831

The whole production was quite Arcadian and primitive, like the infancy of the drama. And when I remembered an opera of Spontini, his *Alcidor*, where everything is imitated in such a very careful and realistic way, where four hundred people sang to represent a huge army, where the anvils were tuned in key, in order to make the forge of the Cyclops visible, where the decorations were changed every moment and each was more glittering than the last—then, after all, the theatre in Lucerne with its bumpy wooden waves seemed to give me more illusion, because here the imagination can have free play and create its own illusions, while there it is oppressed and has its wings clipped.[27]

27. Letter to Goethe, Lucerne, August 28, 1831.

1838

The first evening after my arrival in Berlin we went to the theater to hear Gluck's *Armida;* I have rarely, if ever, enjoyed anything so much at the opera. The great mass of thoroughly trained musicians and singers, ably conducted by Spontini; the splendid house, full to suffocation, the good mise-en-scene, and above all the beautiful music made such an impression on me.[28]

28. Letter to Ferdinand Hiller, Berlin, July 15, 1838.

I went to a performance of *Oberon* last week which was beyond conception; I believe the thing never once went together all through.[29]

29. Letter to Ferdinand Hiller, Berlin, August 17, 1838.

On Orchestras

1828

The orchestra has, to say the least of it, behaved in such an unfriendly manner towards me, that I dare not come forward again as their leader, and it is but natural that I should be unwilling to entrust the direction of my Overture to anyone else, for, as my latest composition it has grown very dear to me. It was a great grief to me to hear that the King's ensemble has refused to be led by me in public, but I cannot feel hurt, for I am too young and too little thought of.[30]

30. Letter to L. Ganz, Berlin, October 19, 1828.

1832

The performers of the Conservatoire in Paris play quite admirably, and in so finished a style, that it is indeed a pleasure to hear them; they delight in it themselves, and each takes the greatest possible trouble; the leader is an energetic, experienced musician, so they cannot fail to go well together.[31]

31. Letter to Karl Immermann, Paris, February 13, 1832.

What is most important and outstanding [in Paris] that I have yet heard, is the Conservatoire Orchestra. Naturally it is the best that can be heard in France because it is the Paris Conservatoire that gives the concerts; but it is also the best that can be heard anywhere. They combined the best musicians in Paris and also took young violinists from the classes; they put one of their directors—a capable and enthusiastic musician—in charge and the orchestra then rehearsed for two years, until they were genuinely a unit and there was no longer any possibility of errors before they risked a performance. Actually, every orchestra should be like this, errors in rhythm and notes should never occur. It is a joy to see that mass of young people in the orchestra, and how they start with exactly the same bowing, the same style, the same deliberation and ardor. Last Sunday there were fourteen [violins] on each side and Habeneck conducted with his bow. One can hear how each player completely fills his place, masters his instrument, knows his part and everything it requires, from memory; in short, that this orchestra is not made up of individual musicians but is a community.[32]

32. Letter to Carl Zelter, Paris, February 15, 1832.

The orchestra in Leipzig is very good, and thoroughly musical; and I think that six months hence it will be much improved, for the sympathy and attention with which these people receive my suggestions, and instantly adopt them, were really touching in both the rehearsals we have hitherto had; there was as great a difference as if another orchestra had been playing. There are still some deficiencies in the orchestra, but these will be supplied by degrees; and I look forward to a succession of pleasant evenings and good performances. I wish you had heard the introduction to my *Meeresstille* (for the concert began with that); there was such profound silence in the hall and in the orchestra, that the most delicate notes could be distinctly heard, and they played the adagio from first to last in the most masterly manner.[33]

33. Letter to his Family, Leipzig, October 6, 1835.

1838
The next day [after my arrival in Berlin] they gave a so-called Beethoven Memorial Festival, and played his *A major Symphony* so atrociously ... the coarseness and effrontery of the players were such as I have never heard anywhere, and I can only explain it to myself by the whole nature of the Prussian official, which is about as well suited to music as a straitjacket is to a man.[34]

34. Letter to Ferdinand Hiller, Berlin, July 15, 1838

1839
I felt quite melancholy at the difference between our sense of music in Leipzig and what was given in Frankfurt; for though it goes on very fairly, and sometimes sounds well, still, as a rule; it seems as if they were playing from sheer weariness, or from compulsion, and vastly little of that zeal and love are apparent in the orchestra which so often prevails among us.[35]

35. Letter to his Sister, Fanny, Frankfurt, June 18, 1839.

Chapter Six

Mendelssohn's Views on the Musical Characteristics of various Countries

Austria

1829

If Vienna were not so confoundedly dissipated, so that I have to creep into myself and write something sacred, I should have made nothing new.

At the Kärnthnerthor one wretched thing after the other is given; a respectable opera has not been heard for years, only Auber, and at most *Guillaume Tell*.[1]

The people I associated with [in Vienna] were so dissipated and frivolous, that I became quite spiritual-minded, and conducted myself like a divine among them. Moreover, not one of the best pianists there, male or female, ever played a note of Beethoven, and when I hinted that he and Mozart were not to be despised, they said, "So you are an admirer of classical music?"—"Yes," said I.[2]

1839

The number of friends that *St. Paul* has gained me is really quite remarkable. I could never have anticipated it. It was performed twice in Vienna in the spring, and they want to have a festival there in November, with one thousand performers ("St. Paul" is to be given), which I shall probably go to conduct. This has surprised me the more, because no other work of mine has ever made its way into Vienna.[3]

1. Letter to Eduard Devrient, Vienna, September 5, 1830.

2. Letter to Carl Zelter, Venice, October 16, 1830.

3. Letter to Karl Klingemann, Hochheim, August 1, 1839.

England

1829

I have much happiness and enjoyment in London, especially when I can shut my eyes to music and musicians, and this fortunately is not difficult. Were I to tell them my opinion of their music they would think me rude, and were I to speak to them of music generally, they would consider me quite mad. So I do not trouble them with my notions, but go about and look at the splendid city and the life in its streets, or row on the river, or buy a bunch of lilies of the valley of some bawling old woman in the crowd, and find in it somewhat more of music than in all the concerts such as I survived yesterday, shall endure tomorrow, and put up with again on Friday.

Strange it seemed the other evening when I heard the Messiah, how all the notes were the same, how the entry of every part was precisely in English as in German, how the music speaks the same universal language, and yet every note spoke loudly that it was an Englishman who played it, and that he did "not care over-much about it." The letter was there, but the spirit was absent, and inasmuch as the letter kills, life was everywhere wanting.[4]

For conscience' sake I am going in a few days to play Beethoven's *Concerto in E flat*. Musicians in London think it impracticable, and say the public will eat me; but I don't think so, and shall play it. [On the other hand] were I this minute to play my *Calm Sea*, etc., to the public they would comprehend it far better than the cultivated circle in our drawing-room. Yet they understand nothing about music, which here is bad and at the worst. Then how is it? Also, by Jove, I play better than in Berlin, and why is that? Because the people have more pleasure in listening.[5]

1830

I can never again expect to meet all together such friends as I had in London. Here in Rome I can only say the half of what I think of my compositions, and leave the best half unspoken; whereas there it was not necessary to say more than the half, because the other half was already understood.[6]

4. Letter to Eduard Devrient, May 19, 1829.

5. Letter to Eduard Devrient, London, June 19, 1829.

6. Letter to his Brother and Sisters, Rome, November 23, 1830.

France

1825

You say, Fanny, that I should become a missionary and convert Onslow and Reicha to a love for Beethoven and Bach. That is just what I am endeavoring to do—But remember, these people [in Paris] do not know a single note of *Fidelio*, and believe Bach to be nothing but a wig stuffed with learning.[7]

7. Letter to his Family, Paris, April 20, 1825.

1831

I feel most uncomfortable [in Paris] to this day. These ways and goings seem to me to smack of the devil; if a man does not pull himself together, he may as well hand over his soul (I mean his musical soul!) to that gentleman in comfort and pleasure. The superficialities are so tempting, people enjoy honors and money and decorations and cheers and orchestras, and lack absolutely nothing—if only they were not such execrably bad musicians! This is what struck me so unpleasantly in Paris; in all kinds of small places in Germany I have met better and greater musicians, but nowhere can they make so much ado about themselves and make people believe everything to the letter. Perhaps this is the point: they never can relax in our country, they have to worry all their lives long and are never appreciated—and yet, they produce WORKS. Here it is just the contrary, and I do not know what to make of it.[8]

8. Letter to Karl Klingemann, Paris, December 10, 1831.

I believe I never in my life passed three such unmusical weeks as these in Paris. I feel as if I never could again think of composing; this all arises from the *juste milieu*; but it is still worse to be with musicians, for they do not wrangle about politics, but lament over them. One has lost his place, another his title, a third his money, and they say this all proceeds from the "*Milieu.*"[9]

9. Letter to his Sister, Rebecca, Paris, December 20, 1831.

The concerts in the [Paris] Conservatoire, which were my great object, probably will not take place at all, because the Commission of the Ministry wished to give a Commission to the Commission of the society, to deprive a Commission of Professors of their share of the profits; on which the

Commission of the Conservatoire replied to the Commission of the Ministry, that they might go and be hanged. The Opera Comique is bankrupt; at the Grand Opera, they only give little operas, which amuse me though they neither provoke nor excite me and the Chapelle Royale is gone out like a light; not a single Mass is to be heard on Sundays in all Paris, unless accompanied by serpents.[10]

10. Letter to his Sister, Fanny, Paris, December 28, 1831.

1832

The musicians in Paris are as numerous as the sands of the sea — all hating each other. So each must be visited individually, and wary diplomacy is advisable, for they are all gossips, and what one says to another, the whole corps knows the next morning.[11]

11. Letter to Karl Immermann, Paris, January 11, 1832.

This, however, is France, and that is why no German city can be compared to Paris. For all outstanding elements to be found in France flow together in this spot, while in Germany they become disseminated. Germany is made up of so and so many cities, but as far as music is concerned—and I believe that is true of all the arts—Paris is France. Here is their Conservatoire where people are educated and where a school is growing up; where all the talents from the provinces must be sent if they wish, in any degree, to complete their educations. For outside of Paris, in the whole of France there is hardly an orchestra worthy the name, and no outstanding musicians whatever. While here we have 1800 piano teachers—and still not enough—there is practically no music at all in the other cities.[12]

12. Letter to Carl Zelter, Paris, February 15, 1832.

Laugh if you choose—my octet is to be performed in a church in Paris, at a funeral Mass in commemoration of Beethoven. This is the strangest thing the world ever yet saw, but I could not refuse, and I in some degree enjoy the thoughts of being present, when Low Mass is read during the scherzo. I can scarcely imagine anything more absurd than a priest at the alter and my scherzo going on.[13]

13. Letter to Carl Immermann, Paris, March 17, 1832.

1838

The rest of the Paris life, in spite of all its wonderful advantages, has very little attraction for me. All that one gets from there in the way of compositions is very modern, very clever, very piquant, but also very cold and too seldom natural. Then everything seems to me exaggerated there, so that I always fancy the musicians themselves cannot really get any good from their music and their manner of life.[14]

14. Letter to Madame Kiene, Leipzig, February 24, 1838

1839

Vanity and outward show nowhere seem to play so prominent a part as in Paris; and the fact that people assume poses not only to become stars, to acquire decorations and wear stiff neckties, but also to reveal their interest in high art, and a soul replete with enthusiasm, does not mend matters. When I read your description of the soiree at Kalkbrenners, I see and hear it all; that anxiety to shine at the piano, that greed for a poor little round of applause, the shallowness that underlies it all and is as pretentious as if such petty exhibitions were events of world-wide importance![15]

15. Letter to Ignaz Moscheles, Leipzig, November 30, 1839.

Germany

1829

Altogether musical prospects in Germany are wretched. Here in London music is treated as a business; it is calculated, paid for, and bargained over, and much indeed is wanting; but the difference between a musical festival here and in Germany shows where the disparity lies. Here, however greedy of gain and calculating they may be, they are always gentlemen, otherwise they would not retain their place in good society, and this is where our court musicians fail altogether. When I think of the musicians of Berlin, I overflow with gall and wormwood; they are miserable shams, with their sentimentality and devotion to art. I have no intention to sing the praises- of English musicians, but when they eat an apple pie, at all events they do not talk about the abstract nature of a pie, and of the affinities of -its constituent crust and apple, but they heartily eat it down. May the devil have his own![16]

16. Letter to Eduard Devrient, London, October 29, 1829.

1830

My Germany is certainly a mad country; it can produce great people and then ignore them; it has plenty of fine singers, and many intelligent artists, but none sufficiently modest and subordinate to render their parts faithfully and without false pretension.[17]

17. Letter to his Family, · Munich, June 6, 1830.

Music is very much run after here, and there is plenty of it, but it seems to me that almost everything makes an impression in this place, and that the impression does not last. It is most amusing to see the difference between a Munich and a Berlin musical party. In Berlin, when a piece of music comes to an end, the whole company sits in solemn silence, each one considering what his opinion is to be, nobody giving a sign of applause or pleasure, and all the while the performer is in the most painful embarrassment, not knowing whether, and in what spirit, he has been listened to. And yet, afterwards, he often finds that people have given all their attention and have been very deeply moved, though to all appearance they are so cold and indifferent. Here, on the contrary, it is great fun playing at a party, because the people can't help talking every minute about what they like; sometimes they even begin clapping and applauding in the middle of a piece; and it is not at all uncommon, when one gets up from playing, to find that everybody has moved, because sometimes, all of a sudden, they want to come and look at one's fingers, and stand all round the piano, or someone wishes to make an observation to someone else, and goes and sits down by him and talks. Afterwards they overwhelm you with compliments and kindness.

The Opera is supplied in the amplest manner, and yet does not produce anything out of the ordinary, because there is no leading spirit to direct the whole thing.[18]

18. Letter to Goethe, Munich, June 16, 1830.

1831

Certainly there is one sure road to fame in Germany, and that goes via Paris and London; still it is not the only one. This is proved not only by all Weber's works, but also by those of Spohr. I am resolved therefore to make the attempt in Germany, and to remain and work there as long as I can and make by living there, for that I consider my first duty. If I find that I cannot do this, then I must leave for London or Paris, where it is easier to get on. If I must, I shall know at least that one is better remunerated and more honored and lives more gaily and at ease there than in Germany, where a man must press forward, and toil, and take no rest. Still, I prefer the latter.[19]

19. Letter to his Father, Paris, December 19, 1831.

1832

I rejoice at the prospect of my return to Germany; everything there is indeed on a small scale, and paltry, if you will, but men live there; men who know what art really is, who do not admire, nor praise, in fact who do not criticize, but create.[20]

20. Letter to Karl Immermann, Paris, January 11, 1832.

People said there was no soul in Madame Belleville's piano playing, so I preferred not hearing her; for what a Berliner calls playing without soul must be desperately cold.[21]

21. Letter to Charlotte Moscheles, Berlin, July 25, 1832.

Berlin pianoforte makers will besiege your door and go down on their knees to you. There are pear-shaped instruments; there are some with three legs; some with a pedal for transposing and with a small writing desk inside; some with four strings, others with only one; giraffe or pocket size; black, white, and green.[22]

22. Letter to Ignaz Moscheles, Berlin, September 26, 1832.

1833

We had last year Solomon and Joshua performed in public in Berlin, and tomorrow there is Samson; but I do not know whether I shall go; fancy that they put wind-instruments to it, during or after the rehearsal, whenever the harmony appears to them not rich enough; a thing Mozart did with the utmost delicacy and carefulness after much study, is now done in a thoughtless hurry.[23]

23. Letter to W. Horsley, Berlin, January 16, 1833.

I know what it is to be a great man amongst the Berliners, now that I am on the eve of my third concert. In the case of my first I had the greatest difficulty to make them accept the whole of the receipts. I played my *Symphony in D minor*, my *Concerto*, and a *Sonata* of Beethoven's, and conducted the *Midsummernight's Dream*. It was crowded, and people were enthusiastic; that is, "heavenly" and "divine" were used much like "pretty well" in ordinary language. And now you should have heard how polite the very people became who had been so obstructive before; how "my noble heart," "my philanthropic views," "my only reward,"—really it deserved to be put into the newspapers. If they had met me kindly at the outset, that would have given me pleasure; now their flow of words is simply a nuisance, and so is the whole place with its sham enthusiasm.[24]

24. Letter to Charlotte Moscheles, Berlin, January 17, 1833.

The only thing wanting is an *ensemble*, which I fear will not be met with in Berlin, as long as sand is sand and the Spree a river.

I have become convinced that Berlin society is an awful monster.[25]

25. Letter to Ignaz Moscheles, Berlin, March 17, 1833.

1835

I am not quite clear as to the state of musical matters in Leipzig. There seems to be plenty of music performed; but how much for the love of the thing, remains to be seen.[26]

26. Letter to Ignaz Moscheles, Leipzig, September 5, 1835.

Altogether this is a strange country. Much as I love it, I hate it in certain respects. Look at the musical men of this place, for instance; their doings are quite shameful. Considering the size and importance of the town, there is really a fine muster of excellent musicians, men of reputation and talent, who might do good work, and who, one would think, would do it willingly. So far that is the good side of Germany. But the fact is, they do nothing, and it were better if they did not live together, and grumble, or brood over their grievances till it is enough to give one the blues. All that is bad, and the German Diet should interfere; for where so many musicians congregate in one place, they ought to be forced by the authorities to give us the benefit of a little music, and not only their philosophical views about it [27]

27. Letter to Ignaz Moscheles, Frankfurt, July 20, 1836.

1837

You once extolled my position here because I had made friends of all the German composers: quite the reverse; I am in bad odor with them all this winter. Six new symphonies are lying before me; what they may be God knows (I would rather not know); not one of them pleases me, and no one is to blame for this but myself, who allow no other composer to come before the public, I mean in the way of symphonies. Good heavens! should not these "Kapellmeisters" be ashamed of themselves and search their own breasts? But that detestable artistic pedantry, which they all possess, and that baneful spark divine of which they so often read,—these ruin everything.[28]

28. Letter to Ferdinand Hiller, Leipzig, January 10, 1837.

1839

My colleagues in Frankfurt are so desperately melancholy, and always talking of musical critiques, and recognition, and flattering testimonials, and constantly thinking about themselves, and constantly fishing for compliments (but these compliments must be genuine; they even aspire to outpourings of the heart!). This is both provoking and sad; and yet (behind people's backs) they can play as mad pranks as anyone. Much as I like Frankfurt for a summer visit, I do not wish to be settled here as a musician, owing to all the above reasons, and many others besides.

I felt quite melancholy at the difference between our sense of music in Leipzig and what was given here; for though it goes on very fairly, and sometimes sounds well, still, as a rule; it seems as if they were playing from sheer weariness, or from compulsion, and vastly little of that zeal and love are apparent in the orchestra which so often prevails among us.[29]

29. Letter to his Sister, Fanny, Frankfurt, June 18, 1839.

1840

Every word, alas! that you write about Berlin and the course of things there, corresponds but too well with my own views on the subject. The proceedings there are far from gratifying, and what strikes me as the most hopeless part is, that all its inhabitants are of one accord on the subject, and yet, in spite of this universal feeling, no change to what is good and healthy is ever effected.[30]

30. Letter to his Brother, Paul, Leipzig, February 7, 1840.

1841

A sorrowful feeling oppresses me when I so surely see, or think I see, that the path lies open, level, and plain, on which the whole of Germany might receive a development which it probably never had, except in years of war, and not even then, because these years of war were years of violence also,—a path on which no one would lose, and all would gain in life, power, movement, and activity; this path is likewise that of truth, and honor, and fidelity to promises, and yet time after time it is never trodden, while new reasons are perpetually found for avoiding it. This is most melancholy![31]

31. Letter to his Brother, Paul, Leipzig, March 3, 1841.

There is a curious misapprehension on your part with regard to the comparison between the two cities. You believe that here in Leipzig we have comfort, domestic life, and retirement, and in Berlin, public efficacy in and for Germany, and active work for the benefit of others, etc.; whereas it is in truth exactly the reverse ... There, all efforts are private efforts without any echo in the land, and *this* they certainly do have here, small as the nest is.[32]

32. Letter to Karl Klingemann, Leipzig, July 15, 1841.

The whole tendency of the musicians in Berlin, as well as of the *dilettanti*, is too little directed to the practical; they play chiefly that they may talk about it, before and afterwards: so the discussions are better and wiser than in most other places in Germany, but the music more defective. Unfortunately, there is very little to discuss with regard to music and its deficiencies; the only thing to be done is to feel, and to improve it; so I have not the least idea how it is ever to become better. In the orchestra (excellent as some individual members of it are) this is, alas! Too perceptible. In operas and symphonies, I have heard blunders, and false notes constantly played, which could only proceed from the grossest carelessness. The people are royal functionaries, and cannot be brought to account, and if the conversation turns on these faults afterwards, they strive to prove that there is no such thing as time, or should be none,— what can I say! *but* item, it goes badly. I have played my trio ten or twelve times here; on each occasion the same mistakes were made in the time, and the same careless blunders in 'the accompaniment, though they were the first artists here who played with me. The blame of this state of things rests chiefly on Spontini, who was for so long a period at their head, and who rather oppressed than sought to elevate and improve the many excellent musicians in this orchestra.[33]

33. Letter to President Verkenius, Berlin, August 23, 1841.

1843

The Berlinese are so in the habit of abusing all and everything, that they are by no means implicitly believed in Germany.[34]

There is much to be praised in these [Berlin] concerts but there are also a few things to be criticized; moreover, there is one small item which they lack and which is generally overlooked here, but which I prefer not to do without, namely an innate vigor and hearty enthusiasm. These people are living, playing and listening in a style of utmost refinement and detachment; no fault can be found with them, but real joy is lacking. I cannot find pleasure in that. There is no dearth of good will, but there is no solid groundwork, no genuine feeling, no sincere conviction. With all this their technical achievement is not to be compared with the perfection heard in Paris; and if our people dream of an *Orchestre du Conservatoire*, they will have to dream on for all eternity. I would not mind that so much, if only the deficiencies were made good by the qualities in which German musicians are infinitely superior – you may call it thoroughness, or honesty, or musical instinct, or decency, or philistinism, or whatever you like but as both extremes are wanting, they fall between two stools in this, as in many another respect. They want to pose as French and they fail to be German.[35]

34. Letter to Eduard Devrient, Leipzig, June 28, 1843.

35. Letter to Ferdinand David, Berlin, December, 1843.

Italy

1830

If Venice, with its past, seemed to me like a mausoleum, where the crumbling, modern palaces and the perpetual reminders of former grandeur made me feel somewhat out of sorts, and sad, Rome's past seems to me like the embodiment of history. Her monuments are exhilarating, they make one feel at once serious and stimulated, and it is a joyful thought that man can erect something which, after a thousand years, can still give enjoyment and strength to others.[36]

36. Letter to his Parents, Rome, November 8, 1830.

Bunsen possesses Bach's *Passion*; he showed it to the Papal singers in Rome, and they said before witnesses, that such music could not possibly be executed by human voices.[37]

37. Letter to his Sister, Fanny, Rome, November 16, 1830.

The impression of Rome as a whole is so solemn and at the same time so inspiring, it fills one's inner being so intensely, that it is in fact precisely as one would like to picture life in ancient time. Other ruins are depressing and melancholy, but these are solid monuments of a glorious past. Whilst in other places everything reminds me of destruction and decay, here I delight in their eternal magnitude and might. Thus the Colosseum and the Basilica of Constantine stand there for men to see what man has created, and feel exalted.

Also I have to be grateful for so much that is not actually music: to the monuments, the paintings, the serenity of nature, which itself is mostly music.[38]

38. Letter to Carl Zelter, Rome, December 1, 1830.

The compositions of Baini are certainly of no great value, and the same may be said of the whole music in Rome. The wish is not wanting, but the means do not exist the orchestra is below contempt.

The Papal singers even are becoming old; they are almost all unmusical, and do not execute even the most established pieces in tune. The whole choir consists of thirty-two singers, but that number are rarely together. Concerts are given by the so-called Philharmonic Society, but only with the piano. There is no orchestra, and when recently they wished to perform Haydn's *Creation*, the instrumentalists declared it was impossible to play it. The sounds they bring out of their wind instruments, are such in Germany we have no conception of.

The people are mentally enervated and apathetic. They have a religion, but they do not believe in it; they have a Pope and a Government, but they turn them into ridicule; they can recall a brilliant and heroic past, but they do not value it. It is thus no marvel that they do not delight in Art, for they are indifferent to all that is earnest.[39]

39. Letter to his Family, Rome, December 7, 1830.

Here again it is the same as with everything else in this place; they may do as they like, build the most execrable houses, plant gardens in the worst taste, perform mediocre music; nature and the past are so rich that everything becomes beautiful and admirable.

What do I care that the wretched bassoonist squeaks in the orchestra, or that the Italians do not genuinely enjoy either painting or music, or anything else? I enjoy them quite enough myself and there are more divine things here than one can grasp in a lifetime. And so the bad music disturbs me very little; though for the sake of truth I must confess that it is really bad.[40]

40. Letter to Carl Zelter, Rome, December 18, 1830.

1831

Any performance of my symphonies in Rome is quite out of the question. The orchestras are worse than anyone could believe; both musicians, and the right feeling for music, are wanting. The few violinists play according to their individual tastes, and make their entrances as and when they please; the wind instruments are tuned either too high or too low; and they execute flourishes like those we are accustomed to hear in farm-yards, but hardly as good; in short, altogether they make a tin-pan orchestra, and this applies even to compositions with which they are familiar.[41]

41. Letter to his Family, Rome, January 17, 1831.

The orchestra and chorus here in Naples are like those in our second-rate provincial towns, only more harsh and incorrect. The first violinist, all through the opera beats the four quarters of each bar on a tin candlestick, which is often more distinctly heard than the voices (it sounds somewhat like obbligati castanets, only louder); and yet in spite of this the voices are never together. Every little instrumental solo is adorned with old fashioned flourishes, and a bad tone pervades the whole performance, which is totally devoid of genius, fire, or spirit. The singers are the worst Italian ones I ever heard anywhere (except, indeed, in Italy), and those who wish to have a true idea of Italian singing must go to Paris or to London. Even the Dresden company, whom I heard last year in Leipzig, are superior to any here. This is but natural, for in the boundless misery that prevails in Naples, where can the basses of a theater be found, which of course requires considerable capital? The days when every Italian was a born musician, if indeed they ever existed, are long gone by. They treat music like any other fashionable article, with total indifference; in fact, they scarcely pay it the homage of outward respect, so it is not to be wondered at that every single person of talent should, as regularly as they appear, transfer themselves to foreign countries, where they are better appreciated, their position better defined, and where they find opportunities of hearing and learning something profitable and inspiriting.[42]

42. Letter to his Family, Naples, May 17, 1831.

I cannot say that I was precisely unwell during the incessant sirocco, but it was more disagreeable than an indisposition which passes away in a few days. I felt languid, disinclined for everything serious in fact, apathetic. I lounged about the streets all day with a long face, and would have preferred to stretch myself on the ground, without thinking, or wishing, or doing anything. Then it suddenly occurred to me that the principal classes in Naples really live in precisely that way; and that consequently the source of my depression did not originate in me, as I had feared, but in the whole combination of air, climate, etc.

The atmosphere is suitable for a grandee who rises late, is never required to go out on foot, who never thinks (for this makes one hot), who sleeps away a couple of hours on a sofa in the afternoon, then eats his ice cream and drives to the theatre at night, where again he finds nothing to think about, but simply makes and receives calls. On the other hand, the climate is equally suitable for a fellow in a shirt, with naked legs and arms, and who likewise has no occasion to move about—who begs for a few *grani* when he has nothing left to live on and who takes his afternoon's siesta stretched on the ground, or on the quay, or on the stone pavement (the pedestrians step over him, or shove him aside if he lies right in the middle). He fetches his *frutti di mare* himself out of the sea, and sleeps wherever he may chance to find himself at night; in short, he spends every moment doing what he likes best, the same as an animal. These are the two principal classes in Naples.[43]

43. Letter to his Parents, Rome, June 6, 1831.

If you suppose that there are any Italian singers in Italy, you are profoundly in error. The prima donna in Rome is a native of Berlin. O misery! she sang execrably, and gave herself as many airs as a horse with bells. All the good singers I have heard in Paris and London, where they are all assembled now, and draw the mediocre ones after them, so that only those lamentably deficient remain at home. Thus it is not to be wondered at that I would rather hear Italian music in Paris.

You can have no conception of an Italian chorus. As I was supposed to be in the land of music, I thought I would try and recognize one good voice amongst the chorus; they were all vile, roar like quacks at a fair, and are always (without exception) a beat before or behind the orchestra. Then the orchestra is composed of wind instrument s out of tune and screaming fiddles, and does not play together.

Could you but hear one of these Italian taught singers, what a total absence of all method they have; how much better and more purely a Bavarian barmaid sings than they; how they ape the little originalities, naughtinesses, and exaggerations of the great singers, and call *that* method.[44]

44. Letter to Eduard Devrient, Milan, July 13, 1831.

In Engelberg was the first time on this journey that I got my hands on a decent organ, for in Italy I did not find a single one in good order.[45]

45. Letter to Goethe, Lucerne, August 28, 1831.

1837
I do so love that enchanting country.[46]

46. Letter to Ferdinand Hiller, Leipzig, December 10, 1837.

1838
You are quite right in saying that it is better in Italy, where people have new music every year, and must also have a new opinion every year—if only the music and the opinion were a little bit better.[47]

47. Letter to Ferdinand Hiller, Berlin, July 15, 1838.

1839
Observe the strange modulations produced by chance in Rome, when one unmusical priest after another takes the book and sings; the one finishing in D major, and the other commencing in B flat minor.[48]

48. Letter to his Sister, Fanny, Leipzig, September 14, 1839.

1840
Mark well the horrible fifths of the Papal singers in Rome when they adorn each of their four parts at the same moment with ornaments.[49]

49. Letter to his Sister, Fanny, Leipzig, January 4, 1840.

Switzerland

1842

He who has not seen the Gemmi knows nothing of Switzerland; but this is what people say of every new object in this unbelievably beautiful country. With regard to this land, I feel just as I do about the best books. They keep on changing with one's inner aspect, present a new phase with every change but always remain towering with the same -loftiness and grandeur.[50]

50. Letter to his Mother, Interlaken, August 18, 1842.

Chapter Seven

Mendelssohn's Views on the Public

1830
I am quite aware of the necessity in every foreign city of playing so as to make myself understood by the audience.[1]

1. Letter to his Brother and Sisters, Rome, November 26, 1830.

1831
I have always found that those pieces which I have written with the least regard for people have pleased them the most.[2]

2. Letter to Eduard Devrient, Milan, July 13, 1831.

1832
The public at these Conservatoire concerts also loves Beethoven devotedly because it believes one has to be a connoisseur in order to love him; but only the fewest can take genuine pleasure in him, and I simply cannot bear to listen to people depreciating Haydn and Mozart; it makes me wild. The Beethoven symphonies to them are a kind of exotic plant, people sniff at their perfume but look upon them as curiosities, and if anybody goes far enough to count the stamens, and finds that they really belong to a familiar species, he is satisfied and lets the matter drop.[3]

3. Letter to Carl Zelter, Paris, February 15, 1832.

1834
Am I not by trade an anti-public-caring musician, and an anti-critic-caring one into the bargain? Only it certainly would be annoying if one never had a chance of hearing one's things performed; but as you say that is not to be feared, let us wish the public and critics long life and happiness,—and me too[4]

4. Letter to Ignaz and Charlotte Moscheles, Düsseldorf, June 24, 1834.

1837
I have never before achieved such a decided effect with my music as in Birmingham, and have never seen the

public so entirely taken up with me alone. And yet there is something about it—what shall I call it—something flighty and evanescent, which depressed and frightens rather than encourages me.[5]

5. Letter to Ferdinand Hiller, Leipzig, December 10, 1837.

1838

If I am not adapted for popularity, I will not try to acquire it, nor seek after it; and if you think this wrong, then I ought rather to say I *cannot* seek after it, for really I *cannot*, but would not if I could.[6]

6. Letter to Ferdinand David, Berlin, July 30, 1838.

An upright man has the hardest stand to make, in knowing that the public are more attracted by outward show than by truth.[7]

7. Letter to Conrad Schleinitz, Berlin, August 1, 1838.

1839

The public applauded tremendously and entered into the Spirit of the *Concerto Pastorale* with more sympathy and feeling than I should have given them credit for. You know I am not generally an admirer of the public; but this time they did try to get at the meaning of the piece, and some of them had really arrived at a right conclusion and understanding.[8]

8. Letter to Ignaz Moscheles, Leipzig, April 4, 1839.

1843

Ever since I began to compose I have remained true to my starting principle: not to write a page because no matter what public, or what pretty girl wanted it to be thus or thus; but to write solely as I myself though best, and as it gave me pleasure. I will not depart from this principle in writing an opera, and this makes it so very hard, since most people, as well as most poets, look upon an opera merely as a thing to be popular. I am aware that popularity is more essential and natural to an opera than to a symphony or oratorio, pianoforte pieces and such like; nevertheless, with these even, it takes time before one stands sufficiently firm to be above all danger of being misled by external considerations, and this leaves me hope that I may yet write an opera with joy, and the good conscience that my principle has not wavered.[9]

9. Letter to Eduard Devrient, Leipzig, June 28, 1843.

Chapter Eight

Mendelssohn's Views on Criticism

1830

It seems [in Munich] to be thought *bon ton* to abuse the opera and the theatre, and to pay a great deal of attention to the critics, who try to earn their scanty daily bread by scoffing and sneering; this again discourages the actors, the bitterness increases on both sides, and thus it happens that there is seldom much pleasure or real enjoyment.[1]

1. Letter to Goethe, Munich, June 16, 1830.

It always makes me furious when men who have no pursuit presume to judge others who wish to achieve something, however small.[2]

2. Letter to his Father, Rome, December 10, 1830.

1835

Recently I was asked to edit a musical review. Nothing seems more unsatisfactory or distasteful to me than a concern of that kind, in which you undertake to suit other people's pleasure and keep all the annoyance to yourself.[3]

3. Letter to Ignaz Moscheles, Düsseldorf, February 7, 1835.

1836

Nothing is more repugnant to me than casting blame on the nature or genius of anyone; it only renders him irritable and bewildered, and does no good. No man can add one inch to his stature: in such a case all striving and toiling is vain, therefore it is best to be silent. Providence is answerable for this defect in his nature. I know well that no musician can alter the thoughts and talents which Heaven has bestowed on him; but I also know that when Providence grants him superior ones, he *must also develop* them properly.[4]

4. Letter to Ferdinand Hiller, Leipzig, January 24, 1836.

1840

You can have no idea of the fuss they make about Kreuzer's "Rheinlied" here, and how utterly repugnant to me this newspaper enthusiasm is; to make such a piece of work about a song, the chief theme of which is, that others shall not deprive us of what we have already got,—truly this is worthy of such a commotion and such music! I never wish to hear a single note of it sung, when the refrain is always the resolve not to give up what you possess. Young lads and timid men may make this outcry, but true men make no such piece of work about what is their own; they have it, and that suffices.[5]

5. Letter to his Brother, Paul, Leipzig, November 20, 1840.

1841

I have always made it an inviolable rule, never to write on any subject connected with music, in newspapers, nor either directly or indirectly to prompt any article to be written on my own compositions.[6]

6. Letter to Professor Dehn, Berlin, October 28, 1841.

Chapter Nine

Mendelssohn's Views on the Personalities of his Day

Auber

1825

You cannot imagine anything more pitiable than Auber's *Léocadie*. The subject, taken from a bad novel of Cervantes, has been made into a bad libretto, and I would not have believed that such a common, vulgar piece could have remained in the repertoire, let alone had any success with a French public who have so much fine feeling and tact. Auber has set music so tame that it is deplorable. I will not even mention that there is no fire, no substance, no life, no originality to be found in the opera; nor that it is pasted together out of reminiscences, alternately of Cherubini and Rossini; nor will I say that there is not the slightest seriousness nor a single spark of passion in it. But a grey-haired man, a pupil of Cherubini and the darling of the public, ought at least to be able to orchestrate, in our times especially, when the publication of the scores of Haydn, Mozart and Beethoven has made it so easy. But not even That. Imagine that there are perhaps [only] three pieces in which the piccolo does not play the principal part! This little instrument [thus] serves to illustrate the fury of the brother, the pain of the lover, the joy of the peasant girl; in short, the whole opera might be excellently transcribed for two flutes and a Jew's harp ad libitum.[1]

1. Letter to his Family, Paris, April 20, 1825.

1831

Do you know Auber's *Parisienne*? I consider it the very worst thing he has ever produced. Auber alone could have been guilty of composing for a great nation, in the most violent state of excitement, a cold, insignificant piece, quite commonplace, and trivial. The refrain revolts me every time I think of it. The words also are worthless. Then the emptiness of the music! By the way, I never saw such a striking identity between poet and musician, as between Auber and Clauren. Auber faithfully renders note for note, what the other writes word for word— braggadocio, degrading sensuality, pedantry, epicurism, and parodies of foreign nationality. Any young poet must indeed be degenerate, if he does not cordially hate and despise such trash; but it is only too true that the people like him[2]

2. Letter to his Family, Wallenstadt, September 2, 1831.

Bach

1832
I have come across a whole book of unknown [Bach] compositions and Breitkopf and Härtel are going to publish them. There are heavenly things amongst them.[3]

3. Letter to Ignaz Moscheles, Berlin, August 10, 1832.

1838
I consider it absolutely necessary to have the name of Sebastian Bach in the program, if only for one short piece; for it is certainly high time that at these Köln festivals, on which the name of Handel has shed such luster, another immortal master, who is in no one point inferior to any master, and in many points superior to all, should no longer be forgotten.[4]

4. Letter to the Committee of the Lower Rhine Musical Festival, Leipzig, January 18, 1838.

1839
Dear Fanny! I beg that among the six great organ preludes and fugues of Bach, published by Riedl, you will look at the fugue Nr. 3, in C major. Formerly I did not care much about them, they are in a very simple style; but observe particularly the four last bars; natural and simple as they are, I fell quite in love with them and played them over at least fifty times yesterday. How the left hand glides and turns and how gently it dies away towards the close! It pleased me beyond all measure.[5]

5. Letter to his Mother, Frankfurt, July 3, 1839.

1840
Until now no outward symbol has betokened the former presence in Leipzig, of the greatest artist this city ever

possessed. One of his successor s has already been honored with a memorial in the vicinity of the Thomas School, which, above all, should have been bestowed on Bach; but as his intellect and his works seem to gain stronger influence now than ever, and as sympathy with these can never become extinguished in the hearts of the true lovers of music, it is hoped that such an undertaking [a proposed Bach monument] may meet with appreciation and assistance from the inhabitants of Leipzig.[6]

6. Quoted by Robert Schumann in "Mendelssohn's Organ Concert," in *Neue Zeitschrift für Musik*, 1840.

Yes! the arpeggios in the *Chromatic fantasia* of Bach are certainly the chief effect. I take the liberty to play them with all possible crescendos, and pianos and fortissimos, pedal of course, and to double the notes in the bass; further, to mark the small passing notes at the beginning of the arpeggios, etc., and likewise the principal notes of the melody just as they come: rendered thus, the succession of glorious harmonies produces an admirable effect on our rich-toned new pianos.[7]

7. Letter to his Sister, Fanny, Leipzig, November 14, 1840.

1842
The monument to old Sebastian Bach is now very handsome. The whole structure, with its numerous elegant decorations, is really typical of the old fellow.[8]

8. Letter to his Mother, Leipzig, December 11, 1842.

1846
The *Double Concerto* of Bach is beautiful, but not brilliant; that of Mozart rather than the other way.[9]

9. Letter to Ignaz Moscheles, Leipzig, July 12, 1846.

Beethoven

1831
The elderly wife of General Ertmann plays Beethoven's works admirably, though it is so long since she studied them; she sometime rather exaggerates the expression, dwelling too long on one passage, and then hurrying the next; but there are many parts that she plays splendidly, and I think I have learned something from her.

In the intervals of our music she related the most interesting anecdotes of Beethoven, and that when she was playing to him in the evening he not infrequently used the snuffers as a toothpick! She told me that when she lost her last child, Beethoven at first shrank from coming to her house; but at length he invited her to visit him, and when she arrived, she found him seated at the piano, and simply saying, "Let us speak to each other by music," he played on for more than an hour, and, as she expressed it, "he said much to me, and at last gave me consolation."[10]

10. Letter to his Family, Milan, July 14, 1831.

1834

I again heard something of Beethoven's *Egmont* for the first time; but it had no particular charm for me, and only two pieces – the march in C major, and the movement in 6/8 time, where Klärchen is seeking Egmont—are quite after my own heart.[11]

11. Letter to his Family, Düsseldorf, January 16, 1834.

Berlioz

1834

What you say of Berlioz's overture, *Les Francs Juges*, I thoroughly agree with. It is a chaotic, prosaic piece, and yet more humanly conceived than some of his others. I always felt inclined to say with Faust:

> He ran about, he ran about,
> His thirst in puddles laving;
> He gnawed and scratched the house throughout,
> But nothing cured his raving;
> And driven at last, in open day,
> He ran into the kitchen.

For his orchestration is such a frightful muddle, such an incongruous mess, that one ought to wash one's hands after handling one of his scores. Besides, it is really a shame to set nothing but, murder, misery and wailing to music; even if it were well done, it would simply give us a record of atrocities. At first he made me quite melancholy, because his judgments on others are so clever, so cool and so correct, he seems so thoroughly sensible, and yet he does not perceive that his own works are such nonsensical rubbish.[12]

12. Letter to Ignaz Moscheles, Düsseldorf, April, 1834.

1835

What you say about Berlioz's *Symphony* is literally true, I am sure; only I must add that the whole thing seems to me so dreadfully slow; and what could be worse? Music may be a piece of uncouth, crazy, barefaced impudence, and still have some "go" about it and be amusing; but this is simply insipid and altogether lifeless.[13]

What Berlioz writes is not music either.[14]

1839

Berlioz's program that you sent me is a very silly production. I wish I could see any pluck or originality in it, but to me it seems simply vapid and insipid.[15]

Cherubini

1834

There is Cherubini's new Opera, *Ali Baba*, for instance, which I have just been looking through. I was delighted with some parts, but in others it grieved me to find him chiming in with that perverted new fad of the Parisians, winding up pieces, in themselves calm and dignified, with thunder-clap effects, scoring as if instruments were nothing and effect everything, three or four trombones blasting away at you as if the human ear could stand anything. Then the finale with their uncouth harmonies, tearing and dashing about, enough to make an end of you. How bright and sparkling, on the other hand, are some of the pieces in his former manner; between *Faniska* and *Lodoiska*, for instance, and this there really is as wide a difference as between a man and a scarecrow,—no wonder the Opera was a failure. To an admirer of old Cherubini it really is annoying that he should write such miserable stuff, and not have the pluck to resist the so-called taste of the day of the public.[16]

1835

Old Cherubini's *Ali Baba* is dreadfully poor and borders on Auber. That is very sad.[17]

---

13. Letter to Ignaz Moscheles, Düsseldorf, March 25, 1835.

14. Letter to Ignaz Moscheles, Berlin, August 13, 1835.

15. Letter to Ignaz Moscheles, Leipzig, November 30, 1839.

16. Letter to Ignaz and Charlotte Moscheles, Düsseldorf, June 26, 1834.

17. Letter to Ignaz Moscheles, Berlin, August 13, 1835.

1839

And old Cherubini? There is a man for you! I have got his *Abencerages*, and am again and again enjoying his sparkling fire, his clever and unexpected transitions, and the neatness and grace with which he writes. I am truly grateful to this fine old gentleman. It is all so free, so bold and bright.[18]

18. Letter to Ignaz Moscheles, Leipzig, November 30, 1839.

Chopin

1834

The next morning Chopin, Ferdinand Hiller, and I betook ourselves to the piano where I had the greatest enjoyment. They have both much improved in execution, and, as a pianist, Chopin is now one of the very first of all. He produces new effects like Pagannini on his violin, and achieves wonderful passages, such as no one could formerly have thought practicable. Hiller, too, is an admirable player—vigorous and yet light. Both, however, rather toil in the Parisian spasmodic and impassioned style, too, often losing sight of time and sobriety and of true music; I, on the other hand, do so perhaps too little,—thus we all three mutually learn and improve each other, while I feel rather like a schoolmaster, and they a little like mirliflores or incroyables.[19]

19. Letter to his Mother, Düsseldorf, May 23, 1834.

1835

Among the new music you are constantly looking through, have you come across anything good? I have not seen anything that I quite like. A book of Mazurkas by Chopin and a few new pieces of his are so mannered that they are hard to stand.[20]

20. Letter to Ignaz Moscheles, Düsseldorf, February 7, 1835.

If the Hamburgers look upon your appearance as an intermezzo between Chopin and Kalkbrenner, let them go to [hell]. I would soon put things into plain language—an intermezzo between mixed pickles, hashes, and fish patties. Kalkbrenner is the little fish patty.[21]

21. Letter to Ignaz Moscheles, Leipzig, September 5, 1835.

I accompanied the Hensels to Delitzsch, Chopin came; he intended to remain only one day, so we spent this entirely together and made music. I cannot deny, dear Fanny, that I have lately found that you are not doing him sufficient justice in your judgment; perhaps he was not in the right humor for playing when you heard him, which can often be the case with him. But, as for myself, his playing has enchanted me afresh, and I am persuaded that if you, and Father also, had heard him play some of his better pieces as he played them to me, you would say the same. There is something entirely original in his piano playing, and it is at the same time so masterly, that he may be called a perfect virtuoso; and as, in music, I like and rejoice in every style of perfection, the day was most agreeable to me.

Sunday evening was really very remarkable, when Chopin made me play over my oratorio to him, and when, between the first and second part, he dashed into his new Etudes and a new Concerto, to the amazement of the Leipzigers, and then I resumed my *St. Paul*; it was just as if a Cherokee and a Kaffir had met to converse. He has also one, just too lovely, new notturno, a considerable part of which I learnt by ear. So we got on most pleasantly together.

My collection of Handel's works arrived before Chopin's departure and were a source of quite childish delight to him.[22]

22. Letter to his Family, Leipzig, October 6, 1835.

1837

Chopin's new things I don't quite like, and that is provoking.[23]

23. Letter to Ignaz Moscheles, Speier, April 6, 1837.

It seems that Chopin came over here quite suddenly a fortnight ago, paid no visits and saw nobody, played very beautifully at Broadwood's one evening, and then took himself off again. They say he is still very ill and miserable.[24]

24. Letter to Ferdinand Hiller, London, September 1, 1837.

I am surprised to hear of Dohler's being lionized. His playing seemed to me very cold and calculating and rather dull. What very different stuff Liszt and Chopin are made of! Chopin has more soul in his little finger than Dohler has from top to toe.[25]

25. Letter to Ignaz Moscheles, Leipzig, December 12, 1837.

1839

He is certainly the most gifted of them all, and his playing has real charm.[26]

26. Letter to Ignaz Moscheles, Leipzig, November 30, 1839.

Czerny

1830

I wish the devil would take the odious vanity that is the order of the day now! There is Czerny, for instance, he thinks of nothing in the world but of himself, his credit, his fame, his money, his popularity. What is the consequence? He is thought little of in Vienna, no longer considered even as a pianist; and although he has constantly, even whilst giving his lessons, music paper and pen and ink at his side, to give forth his ideas when he cannot retain them any longer, even the publishers shrug their shoulders and think "the public is no longer so responsive as it used to be."[27]

27. Letter to Eduard Devrient, Vienna, September 5, 1830.

Ferdinand David

1839

Let me recommend David to you. He is as sympathetic, straightforward, and honest a man as ever was, a first-rate artist, and one of the few who love Art for its own sake. I seldom make music without him, and what I compose he generally hears first.[28]

28. Letter to Ignaz Moscheles, Leipzig, February 27, 1839.

Donizetti

1831

Donizetti finishes an opera in ten days; it is sometimes hissed, but that does not matter, for he has been paid all the same, and he can go about amusing himself. But should his reputation eventually suffer, he would be forced to do real work, which might be disagreeable. That is why he sometimes spends three weeks on an opera, bestowing considerable pains on a couple of arias in it, so that they may please the public. Then he can afford to amuse himself once more, and once more write trash.[29]

29. Letter to his Parents, Rome, June 6, 1831.

Gade

1842

We yesterday rehearsed for the first time your Symphony in C minor, and though personally a stranger, yet I cannot resist the wish to address you, in order to say what excessive pleasure you have caused me by your admirable work, and how truly grateful I am for the great enjoyment you have conferred on me. It is long since any work has made a more lively and favorable impression on me, and as my surprise increased at every bar, and yet every moment I felt more at home, I today conceive it to be absolutely necessary to thank you for all this pleasure, and to say how highly I esteem your splendid talents, and how eager this symphony (which is the only thing I know of yours) makes me to become acquainted with your earlier and future compositions; but as I hear that you are still so young, it is the thoughts of those to come in which I particularly rejoice, and your present fine work causes me to anticipate these with the brightest hopes.[30]

30. Letter to Nicolas Gade, Leipzig, January 13, 1842.

1843

Yesterday we tried over a new symphony by a Dane of the name of Gade. It has given me more pleasure than any work I have seen for a long time. He has great and superior talents, and I wish you could hear this most original, most earnest, and sweet-sounding symphony. I must thank him for the delight he has caused me; for there can scarcely be a greater [one] than to hear fine music; admiration increasing at every bar, and a feeling of congeniality; would that it came less seldom![31]

31. Letter to his Sister, Fanny, Leipzig, January 13, 1843.

Your C minor symphony was performed for the first time Yesterday to the lively and unalloyed delight of the whole public, who broke out into the loudest applause at the close of each of the four movements. To see the musicians so unanimous, the public so enchanted, and the performance so successful, was to me a source of delight as great as if I had written the work myself, or indeed I may say greater,—for in my own compositions the faults and the less successful portions always seem to me most prominent, whereas in your work I felt nothing but pure delight in all its admirable beauties.[32]

32. Letter to Nicolas Gade, Leipzig, March 3, 1843.

Goethe

1821
One would never take him for seventy-three, but for fifty ... He does not strike me as imposing; actually he is not much taller than father; but his bearing, his speech, and his name—these are imposing. The sound of his voice is tremendous, and he can shout like ten thousand warriors. His hair is not yet white, his step is firm, his way of speaking is mild.[33]

33. Letter to his Family, Weimar, November 6-10, 1821.

1830
I thoroughly enjoy the society of the old gentleman. Up to now I have had every midday meal with him, and am invited again today. This evening there is to be a party at his house, and I am to play. It is delightful to hear him conversing on every subject, and asking questions about everything.[34]

34. Letter to his Family, Weimar, May 24, 1830.

Mornings I play to him for about an hour. He likes to hear the works of all the different great piano composers in chronological order and have me tell him how they have progressed. All this time he sits in a dark corner and his old eyes flash. He wanted to have nothing to do with Beethoven, but I told him I could not let him escape, and played the first part of the *Symphony in C minor*. It had a singular effect on him; at first he said, "This arouses no emotion; nothing but astonishment; it is grandiose." He continued grumbling in his way, and after a long pause he began again, "It is very great; quite wild; it makes one fear that the house might fall down; what must it be like when all those men play together!"

During dinner, in the midst of another subject, he alluded to it again. You already know that I dine with him every day; at these times he questions me very minutely, and is always so gay and communicative after dinner that we generally remain in the room by ourselves for an hour or more, while he talks on uninterruptedly.

I then play a great deal, and he compliments me before all these people, and "stupendous" [*ganz stupend*] is his favorite expression.[35]

35. Letter to his Sister, Weimar, May 25, 1830.

When he is gone, Germany will assume a very different aspect for artists. I have never thought of Germany, without heartfelt joy and pride in the fact that Goethe lived there; and the rising generation seems for the most part so weak and feeble that it makes my heart sink within me. He is the last, and with him closes a happy, prosperous period for us![36]

36. Letter to his Father, Rome, December 10, 1830.

Joachim

1844

The bearer of these lines, although a boy of thirteen, is one of my best and dearest friends and one of the most interesting people I have met for a long time. His name is Joseph Joachim. Of all the young talents that are now going about the world, I know none that is to be compared with this violinist. It is not only the excellence of his performances, but the absolute certainly of his becoming a leading artist.[37]

37. Letter to an unknown person, Berlin, March 10, 1844.

Kalkbrenner

1835

Kalkbrenner is the little fish patty ... Kalkbrenner is more like an indigestible sausage.[38]

38. Letter to Ignaz Moscheles, Leipzig, September 5, 1835.

Liszt

1835

What you say of Liszt's harmonies is depressing. I had seen the thing at Düsseldorf, and put it aside with indifference because it simply seemed very stupid to me; but if that sort of stuff is noticed, and even admired, it is really provoking.[39]

39. Letter to Ignaz Moscheles, Berlin, August 13, 1835.

1839

They say Liszt is coming here, and I should be very glad; for notwithstanding his unpalatable contributions to the papers, I am thoroughly impressed both by his playing and his striking personality.[40]

40. Letter to Ignaz Moscheles, Leipzig, November 30, 1839

1840

Liszt's playing, which is quite masterly, and his subtle musical feeling, that finds its way to the very tips of his fingers, truly delighted me. His rapidity and suppleness, above all, his playing at sight, his memory, and his thorough musical insight, are qualities quite unique in their way, and that I have never seen surpassed. With all that, you find in him, when once you have penetrated beneath the surface of modern French polish, a good fellow and a true artist, whom you can't help liking even if you disagree with him. The only thing that he seems to me to want is true talent for composition, I mean really original ideas. The things he played to me struck me as very incomplete, even when judged from his own point of view, which, to my mind, is not the right one …

Liszt's whole performance is as unpremeditated, as wild and impetuous, as you would expect of a genius; but then I miss those genuinely original ideas which I naturally expect from a genius. A mere pianist he is not, nor does he give himself out as such; and that perhaps makes him appear less perfect than others whose talent cannot be compared with his. We are together the greater part of the day, and seem to be mutually attracted. His appreciation of you, and the cordial way in which he expresses it, have drawn me still nearer to him. It is a pity that he should be saddled with a manager and a secretary who, between them, succeeded in so thoroughly mismanaging things that the mildest of Leipzigers were in a rage.[41]

41. Letter to Ignaz Moscheles, Leipzig, March 21, 1840.

There has been too great a hither and thither in the last few weeks. Liszt was here for a fortnight and was the cause of a tremendous uproar in both a good and a bad sense. I consider him to be fundamentally a good, warm-hearted man and an admirable artist. There is no doubt that he plays most of all of them, yet Thalberg, with his composure, and within his more restricted sphere, is more nearly perfect as a real virtuoso; and after all this is the standard by which Liszt must also be judged, for his compositions are inferior to his playing, and, in fact, are calculated solely for virtuosi.

Liszt possesses a certain suppleness and differentiation in his fingering, as well as a thoroughly musical feeling that cannot be equaled. In a word, I have heard no performer whose musical perceptions extend to the very tips of his fingers and emanate directly from them as Liszt's do. With his directness, his stupendous technique and experience, he would have far surpassed all the rest, were not a man's own thoughts in connection with all this the main thing. And these, so far, at least, seem to have been denied him by nature, so that in this respect most of the great virtuosi equal, or even excel him.[42]

42. Letter to his Mother, Leipzig, March 30, 1840.

Fanny Mendelssohn

1847

She seemed present at all times, in every piece of music, and on all occasions, whether of happiness or of sorrow.[43]

43. Letter to Charlotte Moscheles, Baden-Baden, June 9, 1847.

Meyerbeer

1832

I cannot imagine how any music could be composed on such a cold, formal extravaganza as this, and so the opera does not satisfy me. It is throughout frigid and heartless; and where this is the case it produces no effect on me. The people extol the music, but where warmth and truth are wanting, I have no test to apply.[44]

44. Letter to Karl Immermann, Paris, Jaunuary 11, 1832

Moscheles

1832

After so long an interval, it is very cheering once more to meet an artist who is not a victim of envy, jealousy, or miserable egotism. He makes continued and steady progress in his art.[45]

45. Letter to his Father, Norwood, May 22, 1832.

1835

Moscheles came to see me, and during the first half-hour he played over my second book of "Songs without Words" to my extreme pleasure. He is not the least changed, only somewhat older in appearance, but otherwise as fresh and in as good spirits as ever, and playing quite splendidly,—another kind of perfect virtuoso and master combined.[46]

46. Letter to his Family, Leipzig, October 6, 1835.

Mozart

1830

I took the liberty recently of rebuking a certain musician in society here [in Rome]. He began to speak of Mozart and asked me what I thought of the worthy Mozart, and all his sins. I replied, however, that as far as I was concerned, I should be only too happy to renounce all my virtues in exchange for Mozart's sins; but that of course I could not venture to determine the extent of his virtues. The people all laughed, and were much amused. To think that such a person should have no awe of so great a name![47]

47. Letter to his Father, Rome, December 10, 1830.

1831

Another valued acquaintance I made there, is Herr Mozart, who holds an office in Milan; but he is a musician, heart and soul. He is said to bear the strongest resemblance to his father, especially in disposition; for the very same phrases that affect the feelings in his father's letters, from their candor and simplicity, constantly recur in the conversation of the son, whom on one can fail to love from the moment he is known. For instance, I consider it a very charming trait in him, that he is as jealous of the fame and name of his father, as if he were an incipient young musician; and one evening, at the Ertmanns', when a great many of Beethoven's works had been played, the Baroness asked me in a whisper to play something of Mozart's, otherwise his son would be quite mortified; so when I played the overture to *Don Juan*, he began to thaw, and begged me to play also the overture to the *Flauto Magico* of his *Vatter*, and seemed to feel truly filial delight in hearing it: it is impossible not to like him.[48]

48. Letter to his Family, Isola Bella, July 24, 1831.

Neukomm

1832

Neukomm behaves here just as you would expect; he is just the right man for spinsters, for he really is a spinster himself. His extraordinary gentility in contrast to the Berliners, produces an exotic effect, and would be completely wasted if I did not make occasional notes about it in my memory and in my diary. Recently he read me a beautiful lecture on morale; I was admonished to be gay and happy, he had had his black days too and done this and that about them—I just listened patiently, so that when I get to be an old man I will know how to be like Neukomm; but all the time I wished him at the bottom of the sea; he is too boring. Yesterday we practiced his *Ten Commandments,* in the Singakademie; the chorus "Thou shalt not commit adultery" sounded excellent. The girls do not understand what they are singing about, and the married women do not care. To me the work seems terribly dry; but that does not matter for nothing pleases me now. Apart from this, everything is going well; it will be performed in the Garnisonskirche for charity; Spontini and the Army are providing the brass . "Thou shalt not Steal" roars and rolls like thunder, and the composer can be sure of a medal for Art and Science, or some other decoration of the kind. How all this disgusts me—when a chap keeps steering for such goals while pretending he is a philosopher with the highest standards.[49]

49. Letter to Karl Klingemann, Berlin, September 5, 1832.

1834

Isn't it wonderful that a man of such taste and refinement should not be able to transfer those qualities to his music? To say nothing of the fundamental ideas of his compositions, the working out seems so careless and commonplace.[50]

50. Letter to Ignaz and Charlotte Moscheles, Düsseldorf, June 26, 1834.

1837

I found him, as usual, most amiable, and as kind as ever, and may well take example from him in a hundred things. I never met with anyone who combined greater integrity, with calmness and refinement, and he is indeed a steady, true friend.[51]

51. Letter to his Mother, Leipzig, October 4, 1837.

Paganini

1829

Paganini is here; he gives his last concert on Saturday, and then goes direct to London, where I believe he will meet with immense success, for his never-erring execution is beyond conception. He is so original, so unique.[52]

52. Letter to Ignaz Moscheles, Berlin, March 26, 1829.

Rossini

1836

Early yesterday I went to see Hiller, and whom should I find sitting there? Rossini, big, fat, and in the sunniest disposition of mind. I really know few men who can be so amusing and witty as he, when he chooses; he kept us laughing the whole time. I promised that the Cecilia Association would sing the B minor Mass for him and several other works of Sebastian Bach. It will be quite too much fun to see Rossini obliged to admire Sebastian Bach. He thinks, however, "different countries, different customs," and is resolved to howl with the wolves. He says he is fascinated by Germany, and when he once gets the list of wines at the Rhine Hotel in the evening, the waiter is obliged to show him the way to his room, or he could never manage to find it. He tells the most laughable and amusing tales about Paris and all the musicians there, as well as about himself and his compositions, and how he entertains the deepest respect for all the men of the present day—so that you might really believe him, if you had no eyes to see his clever face. Intellect, animation and wit sparkle in all his features and in every word, and whoever does not consider him a genius ought to hear him expatiating in this way, in order to change his opinion.[53]

53. Letter to his Family, Frankfurt, July 14, 1836.

Schubert

1839

We recently played a most remarkable and interesting symphony [the great C major] by Franz Schubert. It is without doubt one of the best works we have lately heard. Throughout bright, fascinating and original, it stands quite at the head of his instrumental works.[54]

54. Letter to Ignaz Moscheles, Leipzig, April 4, 1839.

Clara Schumann

1842

Madame Schumann played Weber's *Concertstück*, and some Thalberg, as beautifully and with as much fire as ever.[55]

55. Letter to Charlotte Moscheles, Berlin, October 8, 1842.

Robert Schumann

1844

I must tell you I have read and heard this new *Paradise and the Peril* of Dr. Schumann with the greatest pleasure, that it has afforded me a treat which made me easily foretell the unanimous applause it has gained at the two performances at Leipzig and the performance at Dresden, and that I think it a very impressive and noble work, full of many eminent beauties. As for expression and poetic feeling it ranks very high, the choruses are as effectively and as well written as the solo parts are melodious and winning.[56]

56. Letter to Edward Buxton, Berlin, January 27, 1844.

Spohr

1839
The influence of Spohr is hardly to be avoided at such a small place as Cassel is; a man of his talents, of his situation in the musical world, and particularly of his very noble and downright character is always sure to exercise a great power over those that come in contact with him. [57]

57. Letter to Mrs. W. Horsley, Leipzig, January 17, 1839.

1841
I could never appear as the opponent of a master of Spohr's standing, whose greatness is so firmly established; for even as a boy, I had the greatest esteem for him in every respect, and with my riper years this feeling has in no way been weakened. [58]

58. Letter to Charlotte Moscheles, Leipzig, March 14, 1841.

Spontini

1829
What would you say to me if I were to implore you not to be carried away by the glitter of Spontini, but to remain true to good music? [59]

59. Letter to Eduard Devrient, London, June 19, 1829.

1834
Have I not always shown respect for Spontini as a musician (certainly not as a man)? [60]

60. Letter to Eduard Devrient, August 2, 1834.

1841
The blame of this state of things [in the orchestra in Berlin] rests chiefly on Spontini, who was for so long a period at their head, and who rather oppressed than sought to elevate and improve the many excellent musicians in this orchestra. [61]

61. Letter to President Verkenius, Berlin, August 23, 1841.

Thalberg

1837

I positively dislike Thalberg's work as regards the composition; and the good piano passages seem to me of no earthly use, so little soul is there in them. I could no more play his music than I could ever make up my mind to play a note of Kalkbrenner's; it goes against my nature.[62]

[62]. Letter to Ignaz Moscheles, Speier, April 6, 1837.

Queen Victoria

1842

Add to this the pretty and most charming Queen Victoria, who looks so youthful and is so shyly friendly and courteous, and who speaks such good German and who knows all my music so well: the four books of songs without words, and those with words, and the symphony, and the *Hymn of Praise*. Yesterday evening I was with the Queen, who was practically alone with Prince Albert and who seated herself near the piano and made me play to her.[63]

[63]. Letter to his Mother, London, June 21, 1842.

Prince Albert had asked me to go to him on Saturday at two o'clock, so that I might try his organ before I left England. I found him all alone; and as we were talking away, the Queen came in, also quite alone, in a house dress. But I begged that the Prince would first play me something; so that, as I said, I might boast about it in Germany; and thereupon he played me a chorale by heart, with pedals, so charmingly and clearly and correctly that many an organist could have learned something; and the Queen, having finished her work, sat beside him and listened, very pleased. Then I had to play, and I began my chorus from *St Paul:* "How lovely are the Messengers!" Before I got to the end of the first verse, they both began to sing the chorus very well, and all the time Prince Albert managed the stops for me expertly—first a flute, then full at the forte, the whole register at the D major part, then he made such an excellent diminuendo with the stops, and so on to the end. Then I rummaged about a little amongst the music and found my first set of songs. So, naturally I begged her to choose one of those, which she very kindly consented; and which did she choose? *"Schöner und schöner"*; sang it beautifully in tune, in strict time, and with very nice expression. Only where, following *"Der Prosa. Last und Mueh,"* where it goes down to D and then comes up again by semi tones, she sang D-sharp each time; and because the first two times I gave her the note, the last time, sure enough, she sang D—where it ought to have been D-sharp. But except for this little mistake it was really charming, and the last long G I have never heard better or purer or more natural from any amateur. Then I was obligated to confess that Fanny had written the song (which I found very hard, but pride must have a fall), and to beg her to sing one of my own, too. "If I would give her plenty of help she would gladly try," she said, and sang *"Lass dich nur nichts dauern"* really without a mistake, and with charming feeling and expression. I thought to myself that one must not pay too many compliments on such an occasion, so I merely thanked her very much; but she said, "Oh, if only I had not been so nervous; otherwise I really have a long breath." Then I praised her heartily, and with the best conscience in the world; for just that part with the long C at the close she had done so well, taking it and the three notes next to it all in the same breath, as one seldom hears it done, and therefore it amused me doubly that she herself should have begun about it. After this Prince Albert sang the Erntelied, *"Es ist ein Schnitter,"* and then he said I must play him something before I went, and gave me as themes the chorale which be had played on the organ and the song he had just sung. If everything had gone as usual, I ought to have improvised dreadfully badly; for that is what nearly always happens to me when I want it to go well, and then I should have gone away vexed with the whole morning. But just as if I were to keep the nicest, most charming recollection of it, without any unpleasantness at all, I have rarely improvised as well. I was in the mood for it, and played a long time, and enjoyed it myself; of course, besides the two themes, I also brought in the songs the Queen had sung; but it all worked in so naturally that I would have been glad not to stop. And they followed me with so much intelligence and attention that I felt more at my ease than I ever have in improvising before an audience.[64]

64. Letter to his Mother, Frankfurt, July 19, 1842.

Wagner

1843

I believe nothing, absolutely nothing, except what I see with my own eyes on the music paper, or hear with my own ears. Unfortunately the case is almost the same with Wagner; I am afraid that a great deal becomes exaggerated in that quarter; and just those musicians whom I know to be conscientious people, increase my fear not a little. Still I have not yet heard any connected passages of his operas, and I always think that they must be better than people say. Talent he most certainly has, and I was delighted that he got that position [Hofkapellmeister in Dresden] even though it won him enemies enough in the course of those few weeks.[65]

65. Letter to Ferdinand Hiller, Leipzig, March 3, 1843.

Part III
Mendelssohn: A Self-Portrait

Chapter Ten

Mendelssohn on his Personality and Character Traits

1829

That I possessed a taste for music and some imagination was obvious; the doctor found afterwards that I was rather covetous, loved order and little children, and liked flirting; music, however, he declared to be predominant.[1]

When I am once convinced that anyone is sincere with me, and that I know him, I put down the fellow as firm and true, and life or what you will may tug and change, in my thoughts he still stands firm and true.[2]

I drove away in my open carriage at furious English speed. I was grumpy to all my unpleasant traveling companions, spoke not a word, but kept quiet, half dreaming, half thinking, half gloomy, just as I think one always does, when one dashes along one's two hundred miles in a mail coach.[3]

1830

I am exceedingly anxious to know numbers of people, especially Italians.[4]

If, in the course of my life, I never achieve anything else, I am at all events determined to be unutterably rude to all those who show no reverence for their masters, and then I shall have performed at least one good work. But there they stand, and see all the splendor of those creations for which they haven't an iota of comprehension, and yet dare to criticism them.[5]

1831

I should infallibly have killed him on the spot, if he had talked to me in such a strain.[6]

---

1. Letter to his Father, on undergoing a phrenology study, London, May 1, 1829.

2. Letter to Eduard Devrient, London, June 19, 1829.

3. Letter to his Sisters, London, September 10, 1829.

4. Letter to his Family, Rome, November 8, 1830.

5. Letter to his Father, Rome, December 10, 1830.

6. Letter to his Family, on the Hermit in Tancred's "Lamentations," Milan, July 14, 1831.

There is a vast deal to do in this world, and I mean to be industrious.[7]

7. Letter to his Family, Engelberg, August 23, 1831.

I beg that you will also look to me in the light of a friend, and not write so formally as to my "counsel" and "teaching." This portion of your letter makes me feel almost nervous, and I do not know what to say.

However wildly the storm may rage without, it cannot so quickly succeed in sweeping away the dwellings, and he who works on quietly within, fixing his thoughts on his own capabilities and purposes and not on those of others, will see the hurricane blow over, and afterwards find it difficult to realize that it ever was as violent as it appeared at the time. I have resolved to act thus as long as I can, and to pursue my path quietly, for no one will deny that music still exists, and that is the chief thing.[8]

8. Letter to Wilhelm Taubert, Lucerne, August 27, 1831.

In Italy I was lazy, in Switzerland a wild student, in Munich a consumer of cheese and beer, and so in Paris I must talk politics. I intended to have composed various symphonies, and to have written some songs, but as yet not a chance of it. Paris obtrudes herself, and as above all things I must now see Paris, so I am busily engaged in seeing it, and am dumb.[9]

9. Letter to his Sister, Rebecca, Paris, December 20, 1831.

1832

People now know that I exist, and that I have a purpose; and any talent that I display, they are ready to approve and to accept. They have made advances to me here, and asked for my music, which they seldom do.[10]

10. Letter to his Father, Paris, February 21, 1832.

I must really describe one happy morning last week: of all the flattering demonstrations I have hitherto received, it is the one which has most touched and affected me, and perhaps the only one which I shall always recall with fresh pleasure. There was a rehearsal last Saturday at the Philharmonic, where however nothing of mine was given, my overture not being yet written out. After *Beethoven's Pastoral Symphony*, during which I was in a box, I wished to go into the room to talk to some old friends; scarcely, however, had I gone down below, when one of the orchestra called out, "There is Mendelssohn!"

on which they all began shouting, and clapping their hands to such a degree, that for a time I really did not know what to do; and when this was over, another called out "Welcome to him!" on which the same uproar recommenced, and I was obliged to cross the room, and to clamber into the orchestra and return thanks. Never can I forget it, for it was more precious to me than any distinction, as it show'ed me that the musicians loved me, and rejoiced at my coming, and I cannot tell you what a glad feeling this was.[11]

11. Letter to his Family, London, May 18, 1832.

At that time [three years previous] I said yes. l am not sure that I should think the same now; but as I said so then, I can no longer draw back, and must keep my word. I am incapable of breaking such a promise.[12]

12. Letter to his Father, London, June 1, 1832.

There are certain faces that cannot possibly belong to an artist, and are so icily chilling that the mere sight of them sends me to freezing-point.[13]

13. Letter to Ignaz Moscheles, Berlin, August 10, 1832.

1833

Think of me as a joyous musician who is doing many things, who is resolved to do many more, and who would like to accomplish all that can be done.[14]

14. Letter to Pastor Bauer, Berlin, March 4, 1833.

Strange that all this should happen at a time which otherwise is so imbued with deep fervor and earnestness. I shall leave this place feeling more solitary than when I came. I have found only my nearest relatives unchanged, my parents, my brother and sisters, and this is a happiness for which I certainly cannot be sufficiently grateful to God. Now that I am—as they call it—independent, I have learned to love and to honor my parents even more than before and with better understanding. But otherwise I see, branching off to the right and to the left, many of those whom I hoped to have going along with me, and yet I cannot follow them on their path, even if I would try to do so.[15]

15. Letter to Pastor Bauer, Berlin, April 6, 1833.

1834

In the evening the Prince gives a ball, which will last till four in the morning, from which I could excuse myself if I were not so very fond of dancing.[16]

16. Letter to his Family, Düsseldorf, January 16, 1834.

There has been dancing for the last fortnight, usually up to five o'clock in the morning, with Prince Frederick taking the lead. I have been saved all these splendors by a bad cold, which has confined me to my room for more than a week. I am getting over it now; but it will serve as an excuse for keeping aloof until the end of the Carnival.[17]

17. Letter to Charlotte Moscheles, Düsseldorf, February 7, 1834.

I must now ask your advice on a particular subject. I have long wished to ride here, and when Lessing recently bought a horse he advised me strongly to do the same. I think the regular exercise would do me good—this is in favor of the scheme; but against it there is the possibility of its becoming an inconvenient and even tyrannical custom, as I should think it rather my duty to ride, if possible, every day. Then I also wished to ask you whether you don't think it rather too genteel for me, at my years, to have a horse of my own.[18]

18. Letter to his Father, Düsseldorf, March 28, 1834.

How could your for one moment imagine that I was annoyed by your showing the text [of his St. Paul to the publisher] Schneider? Why should I take umbrage at that? I hope you do not consider me one of those who, when once they have an idea in their heads, guard it as jealously as a miser does his gold, and allow no man to approach till they produce it themselves. There is certainly nothing actually wrong in this, and yet such jealous solicitude is most odious in my eyes; and even if it were to occur that some one should plagiarize my design, still I should feel the same; for one of the two must be best, which is all fair, or neither are good, and then it is of no consequence.

I know of no feeling more distressing than that of having enemies; and yet it seems impossible to be avoided; at all events, I can say, to my great joy that no one can say that there is one single person with whom I am not on friendly terms, if they will at all permit me to be so.

You say the newspapers extol me; that is always very gratifying, though I seldom read them, either the musical ones or any others; only occasionally English papers, in which there are some good articles.[19]

19. Letter to Pastor Schubring, Düsseldorf, August 6, 1834.

I was lately shown a couple of new French musical papers, where they allude incessantly to a *revolution du goût* and a musical transition, which has been taking place for some years past, in which I am supposed to play a fine part; this is the sort of thing I do detest.[20]

20. Letter to his Sister, Fanny, Düsseldorf, November 14, 1834.

1835

There are times when I feel but a poor mortal, and avoid speaking or even thinking about myself. Such times come upon me every now and then; and having no kind friend here to turn to for sympathy, I suffer more than elsewhere. In such times, to speak of myself and my work, depresses me still more.[21]

21. Letter to Charlotte Moscheles, January 10, 1835.

If I were obliged to undergo an examination as a musician, I am convinced that I should be refused at once for I should not do half as well as I could. The thoughts of a prize, or a judgment would distract my thoughts.[22]

22. Letter to Ludwig Spohr, Düsseldorf, March 8, 1835.

They persist that my "admirable likeness" shall appear and be published by Whitsunday, a project from which I gallantly defend myself, refusing either to sit or stand for the purpose, having a particular objection to such pretensions.[23]

23. Letter to his Father, Düsseldorf, April 3, 1835.

During my musical career, I have always resolved never to give a concert for myself (for my own benefit). You are probably aware that, personally, pecuniary considerations would be of less importance to me, were it not that my parents (and I think rightly) exact from me that I should follow my art as a profession and gain my livelihood by means of it. I, however, reserved the power of declining certain things which, in reference to my favored position in this respect, I will never do; for example giving [benefit] concerts or lessons. In all other relations I shall gladly consider myself as a musician who lives by his profession.[24]

24. Letter to Conrad Schleinitz, Düsseldorf, April 16, 1835.

The idea which you communicate is very flattering for me, and yet I confess that I feel a certain degree of dislike to what you propose, and for a long time past I have entertained this feeling. It is now so very much the fashion for obscure or commonplace people to have their likeness given to the public, in order to become more known, and for young beginners to do so at first starting in life, that I have always had a dread of doing so too soon. I do not wish that my likeness should be taken until I have accomplished something to render me more worthy, according to my idea, of such an honor. This, however, not being yet the case, I beg to defer such a compliment till I am more deserving of it.[25]

25. Letter to Regierungs-Secretair Hixte, Düsseldorf, May 18, 1835.

My first concert [in Leipzig] caused me no perturbation, dear Mother, but to my shame I confess that I never felt so embarrassed at the moment of appearing as on that occasion.[26]

26. Letter to his Family, Leipzig, October 6, 1835.

I strive to do my duty and thus to win my father's approval now as I always formerly did.[27]

27. Letter to Paster Bauer, Leipzig, December 9, 1835.

1836

My father's dearest wish was progress; he always directed me to press forwards, and so I think I am doing his will when I continue to labor in this sense, and endeavor to make progress without any ulterior views beyond my own improvement.[28]

28. Letter to his Mother, Düsseldorf, June 1, 1836.

I would never have thought that I could become such a lion in the musical world through my overtures and songs.[29]

29. Letter to his Family, Frankfurt, July 14, 1836.

1837

I long for a less busy life, in order to be able to devote myself more to what is my real mission: to compose music, and to leave the task of performing it to others.[30]

30. Letter to his Brother, Leipzig, October 29, 1837.

1838

If I were a little more mild, and a little more just, and a little more judicious, and a good many other things a little more, perhaps I too might then have a judgment equal to yours; but I am so soon irritated, and become unreasonable, whereas you love what is good, and yet what is bad appears to you worth amendment.[31]

31. Letter to Ignaz Moscheles, Leipzig, October 28, 1838.

So I am said to be a saint I If this is intended to convey what I conceive to be the meaning of the word, and what your expressions lead me to think you also understand by it, then

I can only say that, alas! I am not so, though every day of my life I strive with greater earnestness, according to my ability, more and more to resemble this character. I know indeed that I can never hope to be altogether a saint, but if I ever approach to tine, it will be well.

If people, however, understand by the word "saint" a Pietist, one of those who lay their hands on their laps and expect that Providence will do their work for them, and who, instead of striving in their vocation to press on towards perfection, talk of a heavenly calling being incompatible with an earthly one, and are incapable of loving with their whole hearts any human being, or anything on earth, - then God be praised! such a one I am not, and hope never to become, so long as I live. Though I am sincerely desirous to live piously, and really to be so, I hope this does not necessarily entail the other character. It is singular that people should select precisely *this* time to say such thing, when I am in the enjoyment of so much happiness, both through my inner and outer life, and my new domestic ties, as well as busy work, that I really never know how sufficiently to show my thankfulness.[32]

32. Letter to Professor Schirmer, Berlin, November 21, 1838.

I have been rather lazy of late. From the measles I dropped straight into so much conducting that I could scarcely do anything else, save take an occasional rest. Still, I have composed a new sonata for the piano and violoncello and three violin quartets.[33]

33. Letter to Ignaz Moscheles, Leipzig, December 10, 1838.

1839
False notes make me savage.[34]

34. Letter to Ignaz Moscheles, Leipzig, February 27, 1839.

I am convinced, from repeated experience, that I totally lack the talent requisite for a practical teacher, and for giving regular progressive instruction; whether it be that I take too little pleasure in tuition, or have not sufficient patience, the fact remains that I do not succeed in it.[35]

35. Letter to Professor Naumann, Leipzig, September 19, 1839.

1840
Latterly I have become quite tired of music, and think I must take to painting once more; but my Swiss sketches are coming to an end, and fain would I return thither to make new

ones, but I already see that there is no hope of such a thing this summer. Hiller lately said that I was like those ancient barbarians, who took such delight in the luscious fruits and the warm sun of the South, that they were always longing for them once more; and there really is some truth in this.[36]

Today I made a resolution over which I am as happy as a bird, and that is, never again to participate in any way in the awarding of prizes at a musical competition. Several proposals of this kind were made to me and I did not know why I was so annoyed, until it became clear to me that fundamentally it would be sheer arrogance on my part, which I would not tolerate in others. I should therefore be the last person to set myself up as a criterion and my taste as incontrovertible, and, in an idle hour passing in review all the assembled competitors, criticizing them, and God knows possibly being guilty of the most glaring injustice towards them. So I have renounced such activity once and for all and since then have been very happy.[37]

Whatever talent I might have shown for speaking the English language or behaving like a gentleman, has been lost in the atmosphere of German petty provincialism.[38]

1841

You must not suppose that I ever act in any affair but from my own conscientious impulses. I invariably strive to do and say nothing but what I hold to be right in my conscience and instinct.[39]

The only thing I regret in your charming letter is that you should have countenanced the strange attempts at making comparisons between Spohr and myself, or the petty cockfights in which, for some inconceivable reason and much to my regret, we have been pitted against each other in England. I never had the slightest idea of such competition or rivalry. You may laugh at me, or possibly be vexed, at my taking up such a silly matter so seriously. But there is something serious at the bottom of it; this pretended antagonism, imagined and started by heaven knows whom, can in no way serve either of us, but must rather be detrimental to both.[40]

36. Letter to his Brother, Paul, Leipzig, February 4, 1840.

37. Letter to his Mother, Leipzig, March 30, 1840.

38. Letter to Charlotte Moscheles, Leipzig, August 8, 1840.

39. Letter to his Brother, Paul, Leipzig, January 9, 1841.

40. Letter to Charlotte Moscheles, Leipzig, March 14, 1841.

1842

Lately I went to a concert in Exeter Hall where I had nothing whatever to do, and was sauntering in quite coolly with Klingemenn—it was already the middle of the first part and there was an audience of about three thousand present—and no sooner had I come in the door, than such a clamor, and clapping and shouting, and standing-up ensued, that at first I had no idea that it concerned me; but I discovered it did when on reaching my place, I found Sir Robert Peel and Lord Wharncliffe close to me, and they continued to applaud with the rest till I made my bow and thanked them. I was devilishly proud of my popularity in Peel's presence.[41]

41. Letter to his Mother, London, June 21, 1842.

1843

I feel more vividly than ever what a heavenly calling art is. For this too I have to thank my parents! At a time when everything else which ought to interest the mind appears repugnant, empty and vapid, the smallest real service to art takes hold of one's innermost being, leading one away from town and country, and the earth itself, and seems a blessing sent by God.[42]

42. Letter to Karl Klingemann, Leipzig, January 17, 1843.

1844

If you are like me, you can hear nothing more welcome about your works than when you are told that you have made progress in them. I know of no more noble aim that anyone could propose to himself, than to give music to his own language and to his own country, as you have done and still design to do.[43]

43. Letter to Professor Verhulst, Berlin, November 11, 1844.

1846

Playing and conducting—in fact, any and every official appearance in public—has grown intensely distasteful to me, so that each time I only make up my mind to do it with the greatest reluctance and unwillingness. I believe the time is approaching—or perhaps is already here—when I shall put all this kind of regular, public performance of music on the shelf, in order to make my own music at home, to compose and let this existence continue, as best it may, without me. I do not believe there is much to be learned from it, and as for its usefulness, I have become convinced that a piece of paper covered with notes—even if it is worthless in itself—is of more use to me, and certainly gives me more pleasure, than 250 rehearsals and performances with excellent success.[44]

44. Letter to Karl Klingemann, Leipzig, December 6, 1846.

1847

Strangely enough, it is almost impossible for me at this time to be with strangers. There is no lack of visitors here, both musical and otherwise; scarcely a day has passed lately without one, or several; but they all seem to me so empty and indifferent, that I, no doubt, must appear at least the same to them.[45]

45. Letter to his Sister, Rebecca, Interlachen, July 29, 1847.

My present mood makes me decidedly disinclined for all publicity.[46]

46. Letter to General von Webern, Interlachen, August 15, 1847

Chapter Eleven

Mendelssohn on his Physical and Mental Health

1829

Imagine that from Sunday morning till Monday evening I dragged myself from one fainting fit to another, out of disgust with myself and everybody on the boat, cursing England and particularly my own "Meeresstille," and scolding the steward with all my might.[1]

I am in very good health: London life suits me excellently.[2]

How much lies between my last letter and this! The most fearful sickness.[3]

I began yesterday to sit up a little … my head is still quite dizzy from this long lying in bed …
Say what you like, body and mind are too closely connected. I saw it the other day with real vexation when they bled me, and all those free and fresh ideas which I had had before, trickled drop by drop into the basin, and I became dull and bored.[4]

You will find me grown thin and whiskered, and much besides, but in certain points the same. It is once again the old story of internal and external.[5]

When I came slowly downstairs and the driver offered me his arm to get into the carriage, an agreeable sensation came over me; but when we turned round the corner and the sun shone on me and the sky did me the favor of being a deep blue, I had for the first time in my life, a feeling of health, because I had never before done without it for so long. It gave me a strange but very comforting sensation and I felt the power of returning health.[6]

1. Letter to his Father, on crossing the English Channel, London, April 25, 1829

2. Letter to his Father, London, May 1, 1829.

3. Letter to his Family, Glasgow, August 11, 1829.

4. Letter to his Sister, London, September 25, 1829.

5. Letter to Eduard Devrient, London, October 29, 1829.

6. Letter to his Family, London, November 6, 1829.

1830

I had the misfortune to be thrown out of a carriage, and was obliged to be six weeks in bed and two months in my room. At last I was able to travel home; but my injured foot, which was very weak, made the journey both painful and dangerous, and I felt so prostrate when I did reach home, that I was condemned to another imprisonment of several weeks.[7]

7. Letter to Charlotte Moscheles, London, January 6, 1830.

1831

On such a day as this my paternal home and those I love are much in my thoughts; my feelings on this point are rather singular. If I feel at any time unwell, or fatigued, or out of humor, I have no particular longing for my own home or for my family; but when brighter days ensue, when every hour makes an indelible impression, and every moment brings with it glad and pleasant sensations then I ardently wish that I were with you, or you with me; and no minute passes without my thinking of one or other of you.[8]

8. Letter to his Sisters, Florence, June 25, 1831.

In the Alps all is more free, more sharply defined; more uncivilized, if you will: yet I always feel there both healthier and happier.[9]

9. Letter to his Family, Isola Bella, July 24, 1831.

Today and all this last week I have gone through one of those dark moods of dissatisfaction with myself. This nearly always occurs when I have done no serious work for some time; in fact, I wanted to compose here, and now I am not able to sit down to work owing to the distractions and dissipations of the life around. I really do not see how I can change it. Either I must retire into complete seclusion and leave all these people alone, or I must look forward to a most disagreeable winter.[10]

10. Letter to Karl Klingemann, Paris, December 10, 1831.

1832

On the day that I received the news of Zelter's death, I thought that I would have a serious illness; and indeed during the whole of the ensuing week I could not shake off this feeling.[11]

11. Letter to his Father, London, June 1, 1832.

Time has not yet adjusted itself properly. I am still hanging between the present and the past; the recollections of my journey are still too vivid and every step I take in these streets or in the garden evokes dim images which I do not know where to place. This makes me feel restless and undecided, more than ever in my life, and since I have been here not one single note has come into my mind. My own stomach rebels again in a most disagreeable manner.[12]

I was very unwell at the time I received your last letter, suffering acutely from a musician's complaint, the ear-ache. A proper letter shall follow as soon as I have shaken off that dreadful fit of depression which has been weighing on me for the last few weeks; then only shall I be able to think again pleasantly of pleasant things. Just now I am passing through one of those periodical attacks when I see all the world in pale gray tints, and when I despair of all things, especially of myself.[13]

There are times when I should prefer being a carpenter or a turner, when all things look at me askance, and gladness and happiness are so far removed as to seem like words of a foreign tongue …
For how to overcome these fits of intense depression, I really do not know.[14]

Since your last letter, old boy, my face has again visibly lengthened and my cheer shortened, because in the last few weeks I have felt so indescribably downhearted and depressed. Where this mood comes from hardly matters, though there are reasons enough. I would have preferred to conceal it from you, and not write at all for a long time, had I not decided once and for all to tell you everything I experience, pleasant or unpleasant, just as it happens. Of course I often tell you days later and by that time it may be all over. But as, at this moment, I am particularly despondent and because writing to you cheers me and eases my mind I know you will gladly grant me this pleasure although I also know how dreadful it is to receive such letters. The greatest contributing cause is the loss of beloved friends; with the death of lovely Miss Robert a goodly bit of my own youth has passed away.

12. Letter to Karl Klingemann, Berlin, July 25, 1832.

13. Letter to Ignaz Moscheles, Berlin, September 3, 1832.

14. Letter to Charlotte Moscheles, Berlin, September 3, 1832.

Moreover, I have been in ill health; I suffered from a terrible pain in the ear and later on from headache, but these things always go together. Then there is the present great quiet and monotony following upon the earlier period of excitement; the stagnation of Berlin, the negotiations about the Academy with which they annoy me more than necessary, and in the end will appoint their Rungenhagen to the post, or God know whom else; and then there is my dull head which repels any cheerful thought—the devil take such a time! I have never lived through a more miserable period.[15]

15. Letter to Karl Klingemann, Berlin, September 5, 1832.

If, on the one hand, I have had two years of pleasure such as is rarely enjoyed, I have had my full share of misery since. You say I ought to put all that into music. Yes, if it were but so kind as to let itself be put; but it whirls and twirls and shuffles about, and is gone before I can catch it.[16]

16. Letter to Ignaz Moscheles, Berlin, September 17, 1832.

I am living much as an asparagus does; I am very comfortable doing Nothing. I shall not know what to say if you ask me what I have been doing ever since I came here. Do you think that mine is a sort of drawing room melancholy such as grown-up spoilt children indulge in? I shall come round again, and by the time you arrive all melancholy will have vanished.[17]

17. Letter to Ignaz Moscheles, Berlin, September 26, 1832.

1833

I have again taken a lively interest in music and musicians, and have composed some trifles here and there; they are bad, it is true, but they give promise of better things,—in fact, the fog seems lifting.[18]

18. Letter to Charlete Moscheles, Berlin, January 17, 1833.

Since I have begun my work again I am in such good spirits that I am anxious to cling to it as closely as possible and make it monopolize every moment that I do not spend with my family. The fact of a period like this last half year having already passed, makes me feel doubly grateful. The sensation is like that of going out for the first time after an illness; and in fact, such a term of uncertainty, doubt and suspense really amounted to a malady, and one of the worst kind, too. Now, however, I am entirely cured; so, think of me as of a joyous musician who is doing many things, who is resolved to do many more, and who would like to accomplish all that can be done.[19]

19. Letter to Pastor Bauer, Berlin, March 4, 1833.

I feel my composition shows progress, and that is the main point. As long as I feel thus, I can enjoy life and be happy; the period of last fall, when I had doubts of myself, was the most bitter I can think of, and that I have ever endured. Would that this mood of happy satisfaction could be hoarded and stored up! But this much is bad, namely my certainty that when similar unhappy days occur again, I shall have forgotten all about this; and I know of no cure, and even you will not be able to help me![20]

20. Letter to Pastor Bauer, Berlin, April 6, 1833.

I am working a good deal for myself and for the outer world, and that, in other words, means that I am happy.[21]

21. Letter to Charlotte Moscheles, Düsseldorf, November 25, 1833.

But if my mind is sometimes troubled, I feel it very deeply, and I do not like to hide it from you. Things are no longer what they were at the time of the *"Liederspiel"* and although I really have completely overcome all feelings of depression at the change, it was no easy task and I still have a very strange sensation when I compare conditions. Only my parents are completely unchanged, or rather, even kinder and less reserved; when I am with them, I miss nothing, and the same thing with my sisters. But outside of our home every step reminds me how the city has stopped dead, and therefore gone backward. Music suffers, people have grown more narrow-minded than ever, the best of them have passed away, others who once nursed fine plans are now happy philistines and sometimes remember the days of their youth.[22]

22. Letter to Karl Klingemann, Berlin, December 26, 1833.

1834

I am particularly joyful today at having suddenly lost a most painful ear-ache that has tormented me these three weeks, and made even hearing difficult; the sound of my piano seems quite a new gift. I caught this ear-ache driving to a concert at Elberfeld, with a frightful storm and rain pelting continually into my ear, and lost it by putting on a blister and letting it draw for forty-eight hours.[23]

23. Letter to Eduard Devrient, February 5, 1834.

You can hardly imagine how much better and brighter I feel for the last two months' work, and how much easier I get on with it; so I must keep it up, and get into full swing.[24]

Since last autumn, when I came here, I have written many other works which brought me into a happy vein, and I cannot wish for a more agreeable position than mine here, where I have both leisure in abundance, and a cheerful frame of mind, and so I succeed better than formerly.[25]

1835

It is the greatest calamity that could have befallen me, and a trial in which I must either hold firm or sink. I feel this now, after three weeks have passed over me, without the sharp pangs of the first days, but all the more surely. A new life must begin for me, or all must cease; the old life is passed away.[26]

No doubt you have heard of the crushing blow that has fallen on my happy life and on those dear to me. It is the greatest misfortune that could have befallen me, and a trial under which I must either strive to bear up or go down utterly. I say this to myself after the lapse of three weeks, without the acute anguish of the first days, but I feel it more deeply; a new life must begin for me, or everything must be at an end; the old life is now severed.[27]

I felt for the first time in my inmost being what it is to suffer the most painful and bitter anguish. The wish which of all others recurred to my mind every night was that I might not survive my loss (because I so entirely clung to my father), a sorrow which of all others from my childhood I always thought the most acute. The loss was also that of my only perfect friend during the last few years, and my master in art and in life.[28]

1836

Would that I were less sad and depressed, for sometimes I do not know what to do, and can only hope that the approaching spring and the warm weather may cheer me.[29]

24. Letter to Charlotte Moscheles, Düsseldorf, February 7, 1834.

25. Letter to I. Furst, Düsseldorf, July 20, 1834.

26. Letter to Eduard Devrient, on the death of Mendelssohn's father, November 19, 1835

27. Letter to Julius Schubring, Leipzig, December 6, 1835.

28. Letter to Pastor Bauer, December 9, 1835.

29. Letter to his Sister, Fanny, Leipzig, January 30, 1836.

I feel like a person walking drowsily. I cannot succeed in realizing the present, and there is a constant alternation of my old habitual cheerfulness and the most heartfelt deep grief, so that I cannot attain to anything like steady composure of mind.[30]

30. Letter to Frederick Rosen, Professor of Oriental languages in London, Leipzig, February 6, 1836.

Such is my mood now the whole day; I can neither compose nor write letters, nor play the piano; the utmost I can do is to sketch a little.[31]

31. Letter to his Sister Rebecca, Frankfurt, August 2, 1836.

1837

It has been a week since I was married. I could not tell you if I tried, how the events of last year have added new prospects of happiness to my life, how all that is good has become doubly dear to me, all that is bad easier to put up with, how happy were the last months, how heavenly the last days![32]

32. Letter to Ignaz Moscheles, Speier, April 6, 1837.

It is quite too lovely here, and every hour of my new domestic life is like a festival; whereas in England, notwithstanding all its honors and pleasures, I had not one single moment of real heartfelt enjoyment; but now every day brings only a succession of joy and happiness, and I once more know what it is to prize life.[33]

33. Letter to his Mother, Leipzig, October 4, 1837.

Just tell me yourself whether I ought not to be satisfied, living here with Cecile in a nice, comfortable house with an open view over gardens and fields and the city towers, and feeling as serenely happy, as calmly joyful, as I have not felt since I left my parent's house. Here I am able to command good things and good-will on all sides.[34]

34. Letter to Ferdinand Hiller, Leipzig, December 10, 1837.

This year, with all it has brought me, has been the happiest of my existence, and I daily appreciate the blessings it has bestowed.[35]

35. Letter to Ignaz Moscheles, Leipzig, December 12, 1837.

1838

I should have written to you at New Year's, … but I was prevented in the most tiresome way by an indisposition, or illness, which attacked me in the last week of the year and, I am sorry to say, has not yet subsided. This has put me in bad spirits, and at times made me so desperate that even today I write only because I see that it is no use waiting till I am better. I am suffering, as I did four years ago, from complete deafness of one ear, with occasional pains in the head and neck, etc.; the weakness in the ear keeps on without any interruption, and as I have to conduct and play in spite of it (I have kept to my room for a fortnight) you may imagine my agony, not being able properly to hear either the orchestra or my own playing on the piano! Last time it went off after six weeks, and God grant that it may do the same this time; but though I summon up all my courage, I cannot quite help being anxious as, till now, in spite of all remedies, there is no change, and often I do not even hear people speaking in the room.[36]

36. Letter to Ferdinand Hiller, Leipzig, January 20, 1838.

I have felt unequal to resume the train of my musical compositions since the measles. You cannot conceive the chaos that accumulates round me, when I am obliged neither to write, nor to go out, for three weeks.[37]

37. Letter to his Family, Leipzig, November 5, 1838.

1839

I have been almost all the time since in so very bad state of health, or rather of mind (and that is the same thing), that I disliked writing, playing, composing, and everything in the world. I cannot say that this indisposition, or what its name may be, has quite subsided at present.[38]

38. Letter to W. Horsley, Berlin, October 21, 1839.

1840

Then came an abominable cold and catarrh, which for three weeks confined me to bed, or to my room, but always in very bad humor.[39]

39. Letter to his Sister, Fanny, Leipzig, January 4, 1840.

I feel so keenly the impulse to make some progress with my daily labors as soon as I am in a happy vein.[40]

40. Letter to his Mother, Leipzig, October 27, 1840.

1841

For a week past such languor seems to creep over me…. I don't know whether this arises from the approach of spring, or the enormous quantity of music which I was engaged in during the winter, and which has fairly exhausted me; for several years past the two always come together. But I believe it is the latter; I have conducted fifteen public performances since January,—enough to knock up any man.[41]

41. Letter to Julius Schubring, Leipzig, February 27, 1841.

1842

I have, however, begun to work again, and that is the only thing which occupies me a little. Happily I have some half-mechanical work to do,—transcribing, instrumentation, and similar things. This can be accomplished by a kind of almost animal instinct, which we can follow, and which does us more good than if we had it not. But yesterday I was obliged to conduct. That was terrible. They told me that the first time would be terrible, but sooner or later it must be done. I thought so too, but I would fain have waited for a few weeks. The first work was a song of Rochlitz's; but when in the rehearsal the alto sang piano, *"Wie der Hirch schreit"* [from Mendelssohn's *Psalm*, Op. 42], I was so overcome that I was obliged afterwards to go out of the room, to give free vent to my tears.[42]

42. Letter to his Brother, Paul, following the death of his mother, Leipzig, December 22, 1842.

1843

During the first days of darkness not even music, or the thought of music, could afford me any consolation; but my old love for it soon returned, and now my little study, with its view on the fields and far beyond, is a refuge, in which I gather fresh strength, and can sometimes feel more cheerful.[43]

43. Letter to Ignaz Moscheles, Leipzig, January 16, 1843.

1844

I employed yesterday and the day before entirely in recovering from my great fatigue, in sleeping and eating; I did not a little in that way, and so I am myself again now.[44]

44. Letter to Karl Klingemann, Frankfurt, July 17, 1844.

1845

Our inner life it is that is worth living; but then that is a very different thing to our outer doings,—something very much better. Conducting and getting up public performances is all very well in its way; but the result, even for the public, does not go far. A little better, a little worse, what does it matter? How soon it is forgotten! And what is it but our inner life, our calm and peaceful moments, that act and react on all this, that impel us and lead us onwards, taking all that public business in tow, and dragging it here and there, whichever way it should go?[45]

I am busy; I feel, for the first time this many a day what it is to live quietly and work, and what happiness it brings to have not only one leisure hour, and now and then a leisure day, but a long series of leisure days before one for work; then I am really happy, and enjoy both the work and the days, music, my wife and children, and myself, which is only possible when, as here, there is no hurry-skurry.[46]

1846

The fact is, my health frequently leaves much to be desired; and all this conducting and performing often fatigues me greatly. At such times I scarcely believe I shall be strong enough to go through a musical festival again.[47]

1847

My family are all well; the happy, unalterably cheerful faces of my children have done me good in these days. I have not yet been able to think of music; when I try to do so, everything seems empty and desolate within me. But when the children come in I feel better and I can watch them and listen to them for hours.[48]

It is so lovely here, and we so much enjoy our regular, quiet life. It has enabled me once more to become often quite cheerful; but when people come, and talk at random about commonplace matters, and of God and the world, my mood becomes again so unutterably mournful that I do not know how to endure it.[49]

45. Letter to Ignaz Moscheles, Frankfurt, March 7, 1845.

46. Letter to Eduard Devrient, Frankfurt, April 26, 1845.

47. Letter to Ignaz Moscheles, Leipzig, February 11, 1846.

48. Letter to General von Webern, Frankfurt, May 24, 1847.

49. Letter to his Brother, Paul, Interlachen, August 3, 1847.

Chapter Twelve

Mendelssohn Describes his Experience as a Performer

As a Piano Soloist

1821

On Thursday morning the Grand Duke, the Duchess and the hereditary Grand Duke came to visit us and I had to play for them. I played from eleven [in the morning] until ten in the evening with [only] two hours' interruption, finishing with the *Fantasy* by Hummel.[1]

1. Letter to his Family, Weimar, November 6-10, 1821

1825

The other day, at the request of Kalkbrenner, I played [on piano] the organ preludes in E minor and B minor. My audience pronounced them both "wonderfully pretty," and one of them remarked that the beginning of the *Prelude* in A minor was very much like a favorite duet in an opera by Monsigny. Everything went green and blue before my eyes.[2]

2. Letter to his Family, Paris, April 20, 1825.

1829

When I mounted the orchestra platform and found it completely filled with ladies who had not been able to find a place in the hall, as well as the unknown instrument, I was overcome with panic; and up to the moment I began I had terrible stage-fright; I think I was actually feverish. But as the gay bonnets gave me a nice reception and applauded when I came in, as they were very attentive and quiet (which with this talkative concert public is a rare thing), and as I found the instrument was excellent and had a light touch, I lost all my above-mentioned tremors, calmed down completely, and was highly amused to see the bonnets become agitated at every little flourish—which reminded me and many critics of wind in a tulip-bed.

It went pretty well and they made a great noise when it was over; also the *Times* has bestowed high praise on me. I was devilishly pleased to find that the public here is good to me and likes me.[3]

I shall play the double concerto in E with Moscheles. Yesterday we had the first rehearsal at Clementi's piano factory. Mrs. Moscheles and Mr. Collard listened. I had no end of fun; for you cannot imagine how we coquetted; how the one constantly imitated the other and how sweet we were. Moscheles plays the last movement with remarkable brilliance; he shook the runs out of his sleeve. When it was over, they all said it was a pity that we had made no cadenza, so I immediately dug out a passage from the last tutti of the first part, where the orchestra has a pause, and Moscheles had to comply *nolens volens* and compose a big cadenza. We now discussed, constantly joking the while, whether the last little solo could remain where it was, since of course the people would applaud the cadenza. "We must have a bit of tutti between the cadenza and the solo," said I. "How long are they to applaud?" asked Moscheles. "Ten minutes, I dare say," said I. Moscheles beat me down to five. I promised to supply a tutti, and so we took the measurements, embroidered, turned and padded, set in sleeves a la Mameluke, and at last, with our mutual tailoring, produced a brilliant concerto. We shall have another rehearsal today: it will be a musical picnic, for Moscheles will bring the cadenza and I the tutti.[4]

1830

Recently, at a soiree given by a Countess, who is supposed to lead in fashion, I had an outbreak. The young ladies, quite able to perform adequate pieces very nicely, tried to break their fingers with juggler's tricks and rope dancer's feats of Herz's; when I was asked to play, I thought: well, if you get bored it serves you right, and started right out with the C-sharp minor *Sonata* of Beethoven. When I finished, I noticed that the impression had been enormous; the ladies were weeping, the gentlemen hotly discussing the importance of the work.[5]

3. Letter to his Family, London, June 7, 1829.

4. Letter to his Family, London, July 10, 1829.

5. Letter to Carl Zelter, Munich, June 22, 1830.

1831

On Monday evening, however, the 17th, at half-past six, think of me, for then we dash off with thirty violins and two sets of wind instruments. The first part begins with the *Symphony* in C minor, the second with the *Midsummer Night's Dream*. The first part closes with my new *Concerto* in G minor, and at the end of the second I have unwillingly agreed to extemporize. Believe me, I do not like to do it, but the people insist upon it.

I was summoned to play before the Queen and the Court; there all was proper and polite, and polished, and every time you moved your elbow, you nudged an Excellency; the smoothest and most complimentary phrases circulated in the room, and I, the commoner, stood in the midst of them, with my citizen heart, and my aching head! I managed however to get on pretty well, and at the end, I was commanded to extemporize on royal themes, which I did, and was mightily commended. What I liked best was that, when I had finished my extempore playing, the Queen said to me that she found it strange, the power I possessed of carrying away my audience, for during such music no one could think of anything else; on which I begged to apologize for carrying away Her Majesty.[6]

I have seldom felt so like a fool as when I took my place at the piano, to present to the public the fruits of my inspiration; but the audience were quite contended, and there was no end of their applause. They called me forward again, but I was annoyed, for I was far from being satisfied with myself, and I am resolved never again to extemporize in public,—it is both an abuse and an absurdity.[7]

Then my turn came to play a solo. I was in the mood to extemporize successfully, and felt that I did so. The guests being now in a graver mood, I took three themes from the previous sonatas, and worked them up to my heart's content; it seemed to give immense pleasure to those present, for they shouted and applauded like mad.[8]

6. Letter to his Family, Munich, October 6, 1831.

7. Letter to his Father, Munich, October 18, 1831.

8. Letter to his Sister, Rebecca, Paris, December 20, 1831.

1832

I played the *Concerto* last Monday in the Philharmonic, and I think I never in my life had such success. The audience went wild with delight and declared it was my best work.[9]

9. Letter to his Father, London, June 1, 1832.

1834

Chopin and Hiller rather toil in the Parisian spasmodic and impassioned style, too, often losing sight of time and sobriety and of true music. I, on the other hand, do so perhaps too little.[10]

10. Letter to his Mother, Düsseldorf, May 23, 1834.

1836

I am very weary and exhausted from yesterday's concert, where, in addition to conducting three times, I was obliged to play Mozart's D minor *Concerto*. In the first movement I made a cadenza, which succeeded wonderfully and caused a tremendous sensation among the Leipzigers. Our second violin player, an old musician, said to me afterwards, when he met me in the passage, that he had heard it played in the same hall by Mozart himself, but since that day he had heard no one introduce such good cadenzas as I did yesterday which gave me very great pleasure.[11]

11. Letter to his Sister, Fanny, Leipzig, January 30, 1836.

1837

I never had such brilliant success, and can never have any more unequivocal than at this Birmingham festival. The applause and shouts at the least glimpse of me were incessant, and sometimes really made me laugh; for instance, they prevented my being able for long to sit down to the instrument to play a pianoforte concerto.[12]

12. Letter to his Mother, Leipzig, October 4, 1837.

1840

Fancy my being obliged to play in public four times last week, and two pieces on each occasion. Last Saturday week, the first Quartet Soiree took place, where pianoforte music was introduced; so I played Mozart's *Sonata* in A major, with David, and the B flat major *Trio* of Beethoven. On Sunday evening Ernest played four quartets at Hiller's; one of them was the E minor of Beethoven, and mine in E flat major. Early on Monday the rehearsal took place, and in the evening the concert, where I accompanied him in his *Elegie,* and in three songs besides; on the following Thursday, Hiller and I played Mozart's *Concerto,* written for two pianos, into which we introduced two grand cadenzas, and at the close of the second part of the concert, we played Moscheles' *Duet* in G major. The Saturday after, I again played with David at the Quartet Soiree, a new rondo of Spohr's, and wound up with my trio. In addition, we are to have a musical soire at D—'s, a meeting of the *Liedertafel,* a ball, etc., etc.; and yet with all this, everyone complains that I persist in living so retired.[13]

13. Letter to his Brother, Paul, Leipzig, February 4, 1840.

1842

I had to play in Exeter Hall before three thousand people, who shouted hurrahs and waved their handkerchiefs, and stamped their feet till the hall quaked. At that moment I felt no bad effects, but next morning my head was dizzy and as if I had had a sleepless night. Add to this the pretty and most charming Queen Victoria, who ... made me play to her; first seven, "Songs Without Words," then the *Serenade,* two impromptus on "Rule Britannia," *Liitzow's Wilde Jagd,* and *Gaudeamus igitur.* The latter was somewhat difficult, but remonstrances were out of the question, as they gave me the themes, of course I was able to play them.

I was received like an old friend and where they played with a degree of enthusiasm which gave me more pleasure than I can say. The people make such a fuss over me this time that I am quite dumbfounded; I believe they clapped their hands and stamped for at least ten minutes after the concerto.[14]

I wished for you recently at a subscription concert. I think I never played the Beethoven G major *Concerto* so well,—my old *cheval de bataille*; the first cadence especially, and a new return to the solo, pleased me exceedingly, and apparently the audience still more.[15]

14. Letter to his Mother, London, June 21, 1842.

15. Letter to his Mother, Leipzig, December 11, 1842.

As an Organist

1830

I again extemporized before the Papal singers. The fellows had contrived to get hold of the most strange, quaint theme for me, wishing to put my powers to the test. They call me, however, *l'insuperabile professorone.*[16]

16. Letter to his Family, Rome, November 30, 1830.

1831

A Mass, by Emmerich, was given, and every note of it betrayed its "powder and pigtail." I played thorough-bass faithfully from my figured part, adding wind instruments from time to time, when I felt bored, made the responses, extemporized on the appointed theme, and at the end, by desire of the Prelate, played a march, in spite of my repugnance to doing this on the organ, and was then honorably dismissed.[17]

This afternoon I played again alone to the monks, who gave me the finest subjects in the world—the Credo among others—a fantasia on the latter was very successful; it is the only one that in my life I ever wished I could have written down.[18]

I also play on the organ every day for an hour, but unfortunately I cannot practice properly, as the pedal is short of five upper notes, so that one cannot play any of Sebastian Bach's passages on it. But the stops, with which you can vary chorales, are wonderfully beautiful; so I edify myself with the celestial, flowing tone of the instrument. I have discovered here the particular stops which have to be used in Sebastian Bach's *"Schmuecke dich, o liebe Seele."* They seem actually made for this melody, and sound so touching, that a feeling of awe invariably comes over me when I begin to play it. For the flowing parts I have a flute stop of eight feet, and also a very soft one of four feet, which continually floats above the chorale. But there is a keyboard for the chorale with nothing but reed stops, so I use a mellow oboe and a soft clarion (four feet) and a viola. These give the chorale in subdued and touching tones, like distant human voices, singing from the depths of the heart.[19]

17. Letter to his Family, Engelberg, August 24, 1831.

18. Letter to his Family, Engelberg, August 24, 1831.

19. Letter to his Family, Munich, October 6, 1831.

1840

On Thursday I gave an organ concert here in St. Thomas's Church, from the proceeds of which old Sebastian Bach is to have a monument erected to his memory in front of the St. Thomas School. I gave it solissimo, and played nine pieces, finishing up with an extempore fantasia. This was the whole program. I practiced for eight days before, so that I could scarcely stand up straight on my feet any longer and walked along the street only in organ passages.[20]

20. Letter to his Mother, Leipzig, August 10, 1840.

1842

Recently when I played the organ in Christ Church, Newgate Street, I thought for a few moments that I would suffocate, so great was the crowd and pressure around my bench at the organ.[21]

21. Letter to his Mother, London, June 21, 1842.

As a Conductor

1831

On my way to the concert at night, when I heard the rattling of the carriages, I began to feel real pleasure in the whole affair. The Court arrived at half-past six. I took up my little English baton, and conducted my symphony. The orchestra played magnificently, and with a degree of fire and enthusiasm that I never heard equaled under my direction; they all crashed in at the forte, and the scherzo was most light and delicate; it seemed to please the audience exceedingly, and the King was always the first to applaud.[22]

22. Letter to his Father, Munich, October 18, 1831.

1832

You would be gratified to see all the little kindnesses and courtesies Habeneck shows me. At the end of each movement of the symphony, he asks me if there is anything I do not approve of, so I have been able for the first time, to introduce into the French orchestra some favorite nuances of my own.[23]

23. Letter to Karl Immermann, Paris, March 17, 1832.

1834

I have just come from the rehearsal of *Egmont,* where, for the first time in my life, I tore up a score from rage at the stupidity of the *musici,* whom I feed with 6/8 time in due form, though they are more fit for babies milk; then they like to belabor each other in the orchestra. This I don't choose they should do in my presence: so furious scenes sometimes occur. At the Aria, *"Glücklich allein ist die Seele die liebt"* I fairly tore the music in two, after which they played with much more expression.[24]

24. Letter to his Family, Düsseldorf, January 16, 1834.

We are now rehearsing the *Wassertrager.* It is quite touching to see how eagerly and hungrily the singers pounce upon every hint, and what trouble they will take if anyone will trouble to teach them; how they strain every nerve and really make our performance as perfect as can be imagined, considering the means at our disposal. Last December I gave *Don Juan* (it was the first time I had conducted an opera in public) and, I can assure you, many things went better and with more precision than at performances I have heard at some of the large and famous theatres; because from first to last everyone concerned threw himself into it heart and soul. Well, we had twenty rehearsals. The lessee of the theater had, however, thought fit to raise the prices on account of the heavy expenses; and when the curtain rose on the first performance the malcontent section of the public called wildly for Signor Derossi and made a tremendous disturbance. After five minutes, order was restored and we began, going through the first act splendidly, constantly accompanied by applause. But lo and behold! as the curtain rose on the second act, the uproar broke out afresh with redoubled vigor and persistence. Well, I felt inclined to hand the whole concern over to the devil; never did I conduct under such trying circumstances. I cancelled the opera which was announced for the next night, and declared I would have nothing more to do with the whole theater. Four days later I allowed myself to be talked over, gave a second performance of *Don Juan,* was received with hurrahs and a threefold flourish of trumpets.[25]

25. Letter to Ignaz Moscheles, Düsseldorf, February 7, 1834.

The week before the *Wassertrager* was given was most fatiguing; every day two long rehearsals—that often averaged from nine to ten hours besides the preparations for the church music this week; and I was obliged to oversee everything,— the acting, the scenery, and the dialogue—or it would all have gone wrong. On Friday, therefore, I came to my podium feeling rather weary; we had been obliged to have a complete dress rehearsal in the forenoon, and my right arm was quite stiff. The audience, too, who had neither seen or heard of the *Wassertrager* for the last fifteen or twenty years, were under the impression that it was some old forgotten opera, which the committee wished to revive, and all those on the stage felt very nervous. This, however, gave exactly the right tone to the first act; such tremor, excitement, and emotion pervaded it all that at the second piece of music the Düsseldorf opposition kindled into enthusiasm, and they all applauded and shouted and wept by turns. It is long since I have had such a delightful evening in the theater, for I took part in the performance like one of the spectators, and laughed, and applauded, and shouted "bravo," and yet conducting with spirit the whole time; the choruses in the second act sounded as precise as if fired from a pistol.

The stage was crowded between the acts, everyone pleased, and congratulating the singers. The orchestra played with precision, except some plaguey fellows who, in spite of all my threats and warnings, could not be prevailed upon to take their eyes off the stage during the performance, and to look at their notes.[26]

26. Letter to his Father, Düsseldorf, March 28, 1834.

I am expected to conduct some operas, and I may have as many rehearsals as I like, so that I had twenty for *Don Juan* (four with the Orchestra). It is true that it costs a great deal of time, and breath, and quarreling. But a good performance makes one forget all the annoyances of stupidity and false notes.[27]

27. Letter to W. Horsley, Düsseldorf, April 3, 1834.

The day after tomorrow I am again to conduct *Oberon*, and shall drive on the orchestra full cry, like an evil spirit.[28]

28. Letter to his Sister, Fanny, Düsseldorf, November 14, 1834.

1836

During the course of this whole winter, my situation has not caused me to pass one disagreeable day, scarcely to hear one annoying expression, whilst I have enjoyed much pleasure and gratification. The whole orchestra, which includes very able men, strive to guess my wishes at a glance; they have made the most extraordinary progress in finish and refinement, and are so devoted to me that I often feel quite moved by it.[29]

29. Letter to his Sister, Fanny, Leipzig, January 30, 1836.

1837

Two months of such constant conducting takes more out of me than two years of composing all day long; in the winter I hardly get to it at all here. At the end of the greatest turmoil, if I ask myself what I have actually accomplished, it is after all hardly worth mentioning. At least it does not interest me particularly, whether or not all the recognized good works are given once more or given better. I am interested now only in the new things, and of these there are few enough. I often think I should like to retire completely and never conduct any more, but only write; but then again there is a certain charm in an organized musical system like this, and in having the direction of it.[30]

30. Letter to Ferdinand Hiller, Leipzig, December 10, 1837.

1839

My present hobby is the improvement of our poor orchestra. After no end of letter writing, soliciting and importuning, I have succeeded in getting the salaries raised by five hundred thalers; and before I leave I mean to get them double that amount. But really you would be touched if you could see and hear for yourself how my good fellows put heart and soul into their work, and strive to do their best.[31]

31. Letter to Ignaz Moscheles, Leipzig, November 30, 1839.

1843

I think the movement might be taken too slow, which I found to be the case at the first rehearsal, until I no longer paid any attention to the notes or the heading, but adhered to the sense alone.[32]

32. Letter to Nicolas Gade, Leipzig, March 3, 1843.

Chapter Thirteen

Insights into Mendelssohn's General Outlook on Life

1826

I intend to start at the beginning of this year, and to devote three years to traveling. The object is not to appear in public, but rather to be musically benefited by my tour, to compare the various views and opinions of others, and thus to consolidate my own taste.[1]

1. Letter to Ignaz Moscheles, Berlin, January 10, 1826.

1829

The other day I went to see Dr. Spurzheim's phrenological cabinet, shown by a young physician. A group of murderers placed in contrast to a group of musicians interested me greatly, and my belief in physiognomy received strong confirmation; indeed, the difference between Gluck's forehead and that of a parricide is very striking; and removes all doubt. But when people want to enter into minute details and show me where Gluck had his bump of music and where his inventive power, or exactly where the philosophy is lodged in Socrate's skull, that is very precarious ground and, it seems to me, unscientific, although it may lead to most interesting results.[2]

2. Letter to his Father, London, May 1, 1829.

I have learnt now that we ought to approach the slightest project shyly and rejoice at the smallest success; for even that depends on fortunate coincidence. People, scenery, hours to which I had long joyfully looked forward, turned out to be cold, unenjoyable, often disagreeable; the smallest pleasures went wrong through mere chance, and great pleasures came to pass for the same reason; and all and everything turned out differently from what I expected, desired, feared. This always has been my experience and always will be. But instead of making me apprehensive or anxious, it inspires me with courage; and far from being fearful for small projects, I take up great ones with confidence.[3]

3. Letter to his Sister, London, September 25, 1829.

If only words were not so cold! especially written words![4]

1830

I had a little annoyance—which, according to my theory is a part of pleasure.[5]

I wish the devil would take the odious vanity that is the order of the day now! By heaven! these people do not know anything beyond their tiresome "I," and that is the reason they are so faint-hearted.[6]

Do not commend what is new till it has made some progress in the world, and acquired a name, for till then it is a mere matter of taste.[7]

1831

I may tell you confidentially that I am beginning to feel a particular aversion to everything cosmopolitan. I dislike it as I dislike many-sidedness, in which moreover, I begin to think I have not much faith. Anything that aspires to be distinguished and beautiful and great must be one-sided.[8]

You must battle your way through the present living mob, before you can arrive at the nobility, long since dead, and those who have not a strong arm are sure to come badly off in the conflict.[9]

It is quite fitting that people should be presented to each other through the medium of music-paper as by a third person in society; indeed, I think that in the former case they feel even more intimate and confidential. Moreover, people who introduce anyone often pronounce the name so indistinctly that you seldom know who is standing before you; and as to whether the man is gay and friendly or sad and gloomy you are never told. So we are better off.[10]

I have always found that the very opposite of what the wise people say invariably occurs![11]

---

4. Letter to his Family, London, November 6, 1829.

5. Letter to his Family, Weimar, May 21, 1830.

6. Letter to Eduard Devrient, Vienna, September 5, 1830.

7. Letter to his Brother and Sisters, Rome, November 22, 1830.

8. Letter to his Parents, Rome, June 6, 1831.

9. Letter to his Family, Florence, June 26, 1831.

10. Letter to Wilhelm Taubert, Lucerne, August 27, 1831.

11. Letter to his Family, Righi Culm, August 30, 1831.

1832
First Motto: "Tell it none but the wise." Second Motto: "Worrying Pays."[12]

1833
Once a man has become callous, he is no longer amenable to kindness and friendliness; callous he remains, and keeps on sinning to his heart's content.[13]

1834
We are surrounded here by disagreeable specimens of pastors, who embitter every pleasure, either of their own or of others; dry, prosaic pedants, who declare that a concert is a sin, a walk frivolous and pernicious, but a theater the lake of brimstone itself. The most deplorable thing is the arrogance with which such people look down on others, having no belief in any goodness but their own.[14]

For thorough self-cultivation, the whole of a man's life is required (and often then does not suffice).[15]

1836
I may indeed congratulate you on the fact that no spurious connoisseurs or *dilettanti* can grope their way into your most favorite thoughts, while you must feel the more secure and tranquil in your own vocation, because arrogant ignorance cannot presume to attack you behind your bulwarks of quaint letters and hieroglyphics. They must at least first be able to criticize; so you are better off in this respect than we are, against whom they always appeal to their own paltry conceptions.[16]

1838
I cannot share your sentiment, that any one profession is preferable to another. I always think that whatever an intelligent man gives his heart to, and really understands, must become a noble vocation; and I only personally dislike those in whom there is nothing personal, and in whom all individuality disappears. Individual failures and strife must not be allowed

---

12. Quoted in a letter to Ignaz Moscheles, Berlin, August 10, 1832.

13. Letter to Charlotte Moscheles, Düsseldorf, November 25, 1833.

14. Letter to Pastor Julius Schubring, Düsseldorf, July 15, 1834.

15. Letter to his Sister Rebecca, Düsseldorf, December 23, 1834.

16. Letter to Frederick Rosen [Professor of Oriental Languages in London], Leipzig, February 6, 1836.

to have their growth in the heart: there must be something to occupy and to elevate it far above these isolated external things.[17]

You are also persuaded that what people usually call honor and fame are but doubtful advantages, while another species of honor, of a more elevated and spiritual nature, is as essential as it is rare. The truth of this is best seen in the case of those who possess all possible worldly distinctions, without deriving from them one moment of real pleasure, but only causing them the more greedily to crave after them.[18]

1839

Formerly I used positively to hate all speculators in art, but now I feel chiefly compassion for them, because I see so few who are at rest; it is a never-ending strife for money and fame, and the most superior talents, as well as inferior ones, join in it.[19]

1840

If we could only preserve through life the fresh, contented, and lofty tone of feeling which, for the first few days on returning from a journey, leads us to look at every object with such satisfaction, and on the journey makes us rise superior to all annoyances,—if we could only remain inwardly in this buoyant traveling spirit, while continuing to live in the quiet of home, we should indeed be vastly perfect![20]

1841

If a thing is not rightly begun it never comes to a good end, and I do not believe that public *tracasseries* can pave the way to public opinion; indeed, I believe that such things have always existed, and always will exist, independent of the *vox populi*, which is the *vox Dei*.[21]

To improve what is already good, or to create what is new and good, would be an undertaking that I should rejoice in, and which might be learned, even if there were no previous knowledge of the subject; but to change what is positively bad into better things, is both a hard and a thankless task.

17. Letter to Conrad Schleinitz, Berlin, August 1, 1838.

18. Letter to Professor Schirmer, Berlin, November 21, 1838.

19. Letter to Karl Klingemann, Hochheim, August 1, 1839.

20. Letter to his Sister, Fanny, Leipzig, October 24, 1840.

21. Letter to his Brother, Paul, Leipzig, January 9, 1841.

I know nothing worse than the abuse or non-use of God's gifts, and have no sympathy for those who trifle with them.[22]

22. Letter to his Brother, Paul, Leipzig, February 13, 1841.

No man should concern himself about another. Whether a person be anything extraordinary, unique, etc., is entirely a private matter. But in this world, everyone ought to be honest and useful, and he who is not so must and ought to be abused, from the Lord Chamberlain to the cobbler.[23]

23. Letter to his Sister, Fanny, Leipzig, February 14, 1841.

1842

It is really difficult to say which, in the present day, should be considered most important; without talent nothing can be done, but without character just as little. We see instances of this day after day, in people of the finest capacities, who once excited great expectations, and yet accomplish nothing.[24]

24. Letter to Carl Eckert, Berlin, January 26, 1842.

1843

I cannot as yet at all reconcile myself to distraction of thought and everyday life, as it is called, or to life with men who in fact care very little about you, and to whom what we can never forget or recover from, is only a mere piece of news.[25]

25. Letter to Karl Klingemann, soon after the death of Mendelssohn's mother, Leipzig, January 13, 1843.

1844

Although I love my art, more from my heart indeed than words can say, there are other things before which even that love must vanish and be silent.[26]

26. Letter to G. A. MacFarren, on the illness of one of his children, Frankfurt, December 8, 1844

1846

The older I grow, the more clearly I see how important it is to learn first and then form an opinion; not the other way around nor both simultaneously. I think that it more than ever the duty of everyone to be very industrious in his own sphere and to concentrate all his powers on accomplishing the very best of which he is capable.[27]

27. Letter to Pastor Bauer, Leipzig, May 23, 1846.

Nature

1831

Hegel indeed says, "that every single human thought is more sublime than the whole of Nature"; but in this place I consider that too presumptuous; the axiom sounds indeed very fine, but is a confounded paradox nevertheless. I am quite contented, in the meantime, to adhere to Nature, which is the safest of the two.

It was singular that while I was in the act of climbing, I thought of nothing but rocks and stones, and the snow and the track; but the moment I saw human beings, all the rest was forgotten, and I only thought of men.[28]

28. Letter to his Family, Lauterbrunnen and Grindelwald, August 13, 1831.

1836

The scenery around Frankfurt pleases me this time beyond everything—such fruitfulness, richness of verdure, gardens and fields, and the beautiful blue hills as a background! And there is a forest on the other side; to ramble in the evening under the splendid beech-trees, among the innumerable herbs and flowers and blackberries and strawberries—it is a true delight for one's heart. I could not prevail upon myself to go to the Rothschilds in spite of their very flattering invitations. I am not in the vein or humor at present for balls or other festivities.[29]

29. Letter to his Family, Frankfurt, July 14, 1836.

1845

I have been again reflecting much upon the furry chestnut-buds, but I do not yet understand quite how such a tree grows. Botany explains it about as well as thorough-bass does music.[30]

30. Letter to Eduard Devrient, Frankfurt, April 26, 1845.

Faith

1831
You reproach me with being twenty-two without having yet acquired fame. To this I can only reply, that had it been the will of God that I should be renowned at the age of twenty-two, I no doubt should have been so. I cannot help it, for I can no more write to win a name, than to obtain a conductor's position. It would be a good thing if I could secure both. But so long as I do not actually starve, so long is it my duty to write only as I feel, and according to what is in my heart, and to leave the results to Him who disposes of other and greater matters.

I firmly believe that a kind Providence sends us all things in due time.[31]

The far summits of distant mountain ranges stretching hither, as if surveying the others. I do believe that such are the thoughts of the Almighty. Those who do not yet know Him, may here see Him, and the nature He created, visibly displayed.[32]

1838
So much in my path has fallen to my share without my having even once thought of it, and without any effort on my part.[33]

1846
May Heaven grant you consolation, and alleviate your grief, and one day permit you to rejoin your son, where it is to be hoped there is still music, but no more sorrow or partings.[34]

1847
A great chapter has now come to an end, and neither the title nor even the first word of the next is yet written. But God will make it right one day; that belongs at the beginning and the end of all chapters.[35]

---

31. Letter to Edward Devrient, Milan, July 15, 1831.

32. Letter to his Family, Lauterbrunnen and Grindelwald, August 13, 1831.

33. Letter to Ferdinand David, Berlin, July 30, 1838.

34. Letter to Herr Velten, Leipzig, July 11, 1846.

35. Letter to his Sister, Rebecca, Thun, July 7, 1847.

Time

1830

Many reflections occurred to me as to so many men of renown gradually vanishing from our sight, and our great geniuses have such homage paid to them after their death, and yet during their life, Lafontaine's novels and French vaudevilles alone make any impression on their fellow countrymen; while we only strive to appreciate the very refuse of the French, and neglect Beaumarchais and Rousseau.[36]

36. Letter to his Family, Rome, November 2, 1830.

1834

What is good, however old, remains always new, even although the present must differ from the past, because it emanates from other and dissimilar men.

In order to guide the movements of others, we must first be in motion ourselves, while reflections cause us to look back on the past, not forward. Progress is made by work alone, and not by talking.[37]

37. Letter to his Sister Rebecca, Düsseldorf, December 23, 1834.

1838

Letters, and passing strangers, and rehearsals, and Heaven knows what all the other things are, which swallow up the day, leaving no more trace than if it had never existed. Truly the most delightful of all things is to be enabled to store up precious and enduring memorials of past days, to tell that these days were; and the most hateful of all things is, when time passes on, and we pass with it, and yet grasp nothing.[38]

38. Letter to his Family, Leipzig, November 5, 1838.

1841

It is curious how certain years elapse, when both time and people seem to stand quietly still; and then again come weeks, when everything seems to run about like billiard-balls.[39]

39. Letter to his Brother, Paul, Leipzig, February 13, 1841.

1843

A thousand thanks for the fact of your being one of those people who do not look upon the memories of pleasant times and happy days as dead, but rather as a living and active influence, just as I do with my whole heart, and have insisted on all my life! It is just because such things remain so unforgotten, so dear and precious to me, and because most people like to forget the past in the present, that I am doubly glad when some one thinks as I do, and takes the past with the present, and rejoices in it.[40]

40. Letter to an undesignated person, Leipzig, April 2, 1843.

Women

1829

A beautiful young English lady who was there, desired to know whether she had a propensity for stealing, or any other crime, and it ended in a phrenological examination of the whole party present. One was pronounced good-natured, another fond of children, this lady courageous, that lady avaricious; and as the aforesaid young creature had to undo her long fair hair to allow the doctor to feel her bumps, and looked very beautiful with her hair loose and when doing it up again before the glass, I gave three cheers for phrenology.[41]

41. Letter to his Father, London, May 1, 1829.

Yes children, you may be scandalized; I do nothing but flirt, and that in English![42]

42. Letter to his Sisters, London, September 10, 1829.

1830

I have been, alas!, making love in Baden, and felt the pains and pleasures; it was hard to part, for it was nice; I may never find it so nice again, but it could come to nothing. This morning, being sure of that, I took my leave.[43]

43. Letter to Eduard Devrient, Vienna, September 5, 1830.

1832

If Klingemann flirts, he is only doing the correct thing, and wisely too; what else are we born for?[44]

44. Letter to Charlotte Moscheles, Berlin, September 3, 1832.

1834

Yes, certainly, my horse is more attractive than all the young ladies I knew in Berlin, it is so glossy and brown; then it looks so healthy and so very good-natured (and good-nature, everyone knows, is not exactly what the Berlinese are noted for). However, I do not forswear marriage, for my father has prophesied that I shall never marry. And then really there are not enough pretty girls here; after all, one doesn't want to be composing fugues and chorales all day long.[45]

1836

The present period is a very strange one, for I am more desperately in love than I ever was in my life before, and I do not know what to do. I leave Frankfurt the day after tomorrow, but I feel as if it would cost me my life. At any rate I intend to return here and see this charming girl once more before I go back to Leipzig. But I have not an idea whether she likes me or not, and I do not know what to do to make her like me, as I have already said. But one thing is certain, that to her I owe the first real happiness I have enjoyed this year, and now I feel fresh and hopeful again for the first time.[46]

When I have seen this charming girl again, I hope the suspense will soon be over, and I shall know whether we are to be anything—or rather everything—to each other, or not; at present I really know very little of her, and she of me, so I cannot answer all your questions about her. This much I can tell you, that she made my stay at Frankfurt very happy, just when I needed a little happiness and did not expect to get it, that her Christian name is Cecile, and that I love her very much.[47]

Teaching

1831

Every day [in Munich] I give little Mademoiselle L. an hour's instruction in double counterpoint, and four-part composition, etc., which makes me realize more than ever the stupidity and confusion of most masters and books on the subject; for nothing can be clearer than the whole thing when properly explained.[48]

---

45. Letter to Ignaz and Charlotte Moscheles, Düsseldorf, June 26, 1834.

46. Letter to his Sister Rebecca, Frankfurt, July 24, 1836.

47. Letter to his Mother, The Hague, August 9, 1836.

48. Letter to his Family, Munich, October 6, 1831.

1834

A young musician has just been here with an atrocious fugue for me to look through; also another native genius who feels an impulse to write chorales, enough to make one turn yellow with impatience; and yet he has written chorales ever since I came here, the last always worse than the one before it; and as we go on being vexed with one another, there are some lovely scenes, he not being able to understand that I still find his compositions bad, and I that he has not improved them. I am, however, the very type of a good Cantor, and preach so much to the point that it is great fun to hear me.[49]

49. Letter to Charlotte Moscheles, Düsseldorf, May 14, 1834.

1839

I am convinced, from repeated experience, that I am totally deficient in the talent requisite for a practical teacher, and for giving regular progressive instruction; whether it be that I take too little pleasure in tuition, or have not sufficient patience for it, I cannot tell, but, in short, I do not succeed in it. Occasionally, indeed, young people have stayed with me, but any improvement they have derived was solely from our studying music together, from unreserved intercourse, or casual conversation on various subjects, and also from discussions; and none of these things are compatible with actual teaching. Now the question is, whether in such early youth a consecutive, unremitting, strict course of discipline be not of more value than all the rest? It also appears to me that the estrangement of your son from the paternal roof just at his age forms a second, and not less important, objection. Where the rudiments of education are not wholly lacking, then I consider that the vicinity of his parents, and the prosecution of the usual elements of study, the acquirement of languages, and the various branches of scholarship and science, are of more value to the boy than a one-sided, even though more perfect, cultivation of his genius. In any event such genius is sure to force its way to the light, and to shape its course accordingly, and in riper years will submit to no other permanent vocation, so that the early acquired treasures of interest, and the hours enjoyed in early youth under the roof of a parent, become doubly dear. I speak in this strain from my own experience, for I can well remember that in my fifteenth year there was a question as to my studying with Cherubini in Paris, and I know how grateful I was to my father at this time, and often since, that he at last gave up the idea, and kept me with himself.

I quite agree that it is most essential to cultivate pianoforte playing at present as much as possible, and not to fail in studying Cramer's exercises assiduously and steadily; but along with this daily training on the piano, two hours a week devoted to thorough-bass might be useful, as such a variety would be a pleasant change, rather than an interruption. The latter study indeed ought to be pursued in an easy and almost playful manner, and chiefly the practical part, that of deciphering and playing figured bass; these are the main points, and can be entirely mastered in a short time; but the sooner it is begun, the sooner is it got quit of, and this is always a relief with such dry things.[50]

50. Letter to Professor Naumann, Leipzig, September 19, 1839.

1840

For a long time, music has been indigenous to this country, and just that trend which must lie nearest the heart of every ardent and thoughtful friend of art, namely the feeling for what is true and genuine, has always been able to strike roots in this soil. Such universal sympathy is certainly neither accidental nor has it been without important results for general education. Music has thus become an important factor—not a mere fleeting pleasure, but a spiritual and intellectual necessity. Whoever has a sincere interest in this art must eagerly desire to see its future in this land established on the most solid foundations possible. But the positive, and technically materialistic tendencies of the present day render the preservation of a genuine sense of art, and it further development, a doubly important, but also a doubly difficult task. It seems that this can be achieved only by working from the ground up; and as the expansion of sound instruction is the best mode of preserving every species of intellectual development, so it certainly is with music, too. If we had a good Music Academy which embraced all the various branches of this art, and taught them from one sole point of view, merely as the means to a higher end, and guided all its students as far as possible toward this goal, then this practical, materialistic tendency which, alas! can number, even among our artists, many influential followers, might yet be effectually checked. Mere private' instruction, which once bore much good fruit, also for life in general, now, for many reasons, no longer suffices. Formerly, music students who learned to play various instruments were to be found in every class of society, whereas now the number of amateurs has become more and more reduced and those that are left confine themselves preferably to one instrument, the piano. The students who desire further instruction are almost invariably those who intend to devote themselves to this profession but who lack the means to pay for good private lessons. It is true that the best talents are often to be found amongst them, but, on the other hand, teachers are seldom placed in such fortunate circumstances as to be able to devote their time, without remuneration, to the training of even the greatest talents; thus both sides suffer; the former are deprived of the longed-for instruction, and the latter of the chance to impart their knowledge and keep its influence alive. A public institution would, therefore, just now be important to teachers as well as to pupils. These latter would be given the means of cultivating abilities which otherwise would often be wasted. But for the teachers of music it would be equally important; for to work in a group which has a common point of view and a common goal is the best means of preventing indifference and isolation, whose unfruitfulness these days can become genuinely harmful all too quickly.[51]

51. Letter to the Kreisdirektor von Falkenstein, Leipzig, April 8, 1840.

1841

Remarkable, very remarkable, these statutes of the Berlin Academy are, especially those of the school for composition. Imagine! Out of eleven different branches of instruction which they have instituted, seven are positively useless, and indeed preposterous. What do you think of the following, among others? Nr. 8: "The relation Music bears to the other arts, especially to the *plastic* and to the stage"; and also Nr. 11: "A guide to the spiritual and worldly Drama." I formerly read these things in the Government paper, and laughed at them; but when a grave minister or official actually sends such stuff, it is pitiable.[52]

52. Letter to his Brother, Paul, Leipzig, February 13, 1841.

It is proposed to establish a German Music Academy in Berlin, to concentrate in one common focus the now isolated efforts in the sphere of instruction in art, in order to guide rising artists in a solid and earnest direction, thus imparting to the musical sense of the nation a new and more energetic impetus; for this purpose, on one side, the already existing institutes and their members must be concentrated, and on the other, the aid of new ones must be called in.

Among the former may be reckoned the various Royal Academies for musical instruction, which must be united with this Musical Academy, and carried on as branches of the same, with greater or less modifications, in *one* sense and in *one* direction. In these are included, for example, the Institute for Students of the Royal Orchestra; the Organ Institute; that of the Theater for instruction in singing, declamation, etc. Further, the members of the Royal Kapelle must be required to give instruction on their various instruments. A suitable locality can no doubt be found among the royal buildings, and also a library, with the requisite old and new musical works, scores, and books.

The new appointments to consist of: (1) A head teacher of composition; the best that can be found in Germany, to give regular instructions in theory, thorough-bass, counterpoint, and fugues. (2) A head teacher of solo singing; also the best to be had in Germany. (3) A head teacher of choral singing, who should strive to acquire personal influence over the scholars under his care, by good pianoforte playing and steady direction. (4) A head teacher of pianoforte playing, for which office a man of the most unquestionable talent and reputation must alone be selected. The other teachers for these departments could be found in Berlin itself; nor would there be any difficulty in procuring teachers of Aesthetics, the history of music, etc.

The complete course to last three years; the scholars, after previous examination, to be instructed gratis; no prize works to be admitted but at stated periods; all the works of the scholars, from the time of their admission, to be collected and criticized in connection with each other, and subsequently a prize (probably consisting of a sum sufficient for a long journey through Germany, Italy, France, and England) is to be adjudged accordingly. Every winter a certain number of concerts to take place, in which all the teachers (including the above-named members of the Royal Kapelle) must co-operate, and by which, through the selection of the music, as well as by its execution, direct influence may be gained over the majority of the public.

The following principle must serve as a basis for the whole Institute: that every sphere of art can only elevate itself above a mere handicraft, by being devoted to the expression of lofty thought, along with the utmost possible technical finish, and a pure and intellectual aim; that also solidity, precision, and strict discipline in teaching and learning should be considered the first law, thus not falling short in this respect of any handicraft; that in every department, all teaching and learning should be exclusively devoted to the thoughts intended to be expressed, and to that more elevated mood, to which technical perfection in art must ever be subordinate.[53]

53. "Memorandum on the Music Academy to be Established in Berlin," Berlin, May, 1841.

1843

The pupils all want to compose and to theorize, whilst I believe that the principal thing that can and ought to be taught is sound practical work,—sound playing and keeping time, sound knowledge of sound music, etc. Out of that, all other knowledge grows of itself; and what is beyond is not a matter of teaching, but must come as a gift from above.[54]

54. Letter to Ignaz Moscheles, Leipzig, April 30, 1843.

1846

It is difficult to fix the terms for your teaching piano lessons, even approximately, for there is no precedent in Leipzig to go by. Madame Schumann-Wieck asked two thalers, but at that price found but few pupils, and those mostly among foreigners spending a short time here.[55]

55. Letter to Ignaz Moscheles, Leipzig, January 17, 1846. With respect to the relative value of Madame Schumann's fee, Mendelssohn also cites the annual rent of a seven or eight room apartment at 350 thalers, a good cook at 40 thalers per year and a housemaid at thirty-two.

Painting

1830

I was little pleased with the painters at Munich. They are wanting in the first quality that I think an artist ought to have, and that is reverence. They speak about Peter Paul Rubens as if he were one of them, or indeed scarcely so high; and think they glorify Cornelius when they arrogantly disparage another great artist, whose worst picture they will never understand.[56]

During the very first days of my arrival I discovered a few masterpieces which mean so much to me that I study them a couple of hours every day. There are three pictures by Titian. The "Presentation of Mary as a Child in the Temple"; the "Assumption of the Virgin"; and the "Entombment of Christ." There is also a portrait by Giorgione, representing a girl with a zither in her hand, lost in thought, and gazing out of the picture in serious meditation (she is apparently about to begin a song, and you feel as if you must do the same); besides many others. To see these alone would be worth a journey to Venice; for the opulence, power, and devotion of the great men who painted these pictures, seem to emanate from them afresh as often as you gaze at their works, and I do not much regret that I have heard scarcely any music here as yet; for I suppose I must not include the music of the angels in the "Assumption," encircling Mary with joyous shouts of welcome, one gaily beating the tambourine, a couple of others blowing away on strange crooked flutes, whilst another charming group is singing—or the music floating in the thoughts of the player ... nothing inspires me with more solemn awe than, when on the very spot for which they were originally designed and painted, those old pictures with their mighty figures, gradually steal forth out of the darkness in which the long lapse of time has veiled them.[57]

I believe that whoever finds the most beauties in Titian, is sure to be most in the right, for he was a glorious man.

A pleasing emotion seizes me, when I see for the first time some immortal work, and the pervading idea and chief impression it inspires.[58]

56. Letter to Eduard Devrient, Vienna, September 5, 1830.

57. Letter to Carl Zelter, Venice, October 16, 1830.

58. Letter to his Family, Rome, November 8, 1830.

1839

Comparison between the head and its production, between the man's work and his exterior,—the artist and his portrait: Titian, vigorous and royal; Domenichino, precise, bright, very astute, and buoyant; Guido, pale dignified, masterly, keen; Lanfranco, a grotesque mask; Leonello Spada, a good-natured *fanfaron* and a reveller; Annibale Carracci, peeping and prying; the two Caraccis, like the members of a guild; Caravaggio, rather commonplace and cat-like; Guercino, handsome and affected, melancholy and dark; Bellini the red-haired, the stern, old-fashioned teacher; Giorgione, chivalrous, fantastic, serene, and clear; Leonardo da Vinci, the lion; in the middle, the fragile, heavenly Raphael, and over him Michael Angelo, ugly, vigorous, malignant; Carlo Dolce, a coxcomb; Gerard Dow, a mere appendage among his kitchen utensils, etc.[59]

59. Letter to his Sister, Fanny, Leipzig, September 14, 1839.

Literature

1831

I compared the fire and poetry displayed in every description contained in these letters of Napoleon with the Directoire with the eloquence of the present day, which leaves you so terribly cold and is so obviously prosaic in all its philanthropic views, and so lame—where I notice plenty of *fanfaronnade,* but no genuine youth—and it seemed to me that a great epoch has passed away for ever.[60]

60. Letter to his Parents, Prieure de Chamonix, July, 1831.

My heart is so full that I must tell you about it. In this enchanting valley I have just taken up Shiller's "Wilhelm Tell," and read half of the first scene; there is surely no art like our German one! Heaven knows why it is so; but I do think that no other nation could fully comprehend such an opening scene, far less be able to compose it. This is what I call a poem, and an opening; pure, clear verse, in which the lake, smooth as a mirror, and everything else is so vividly described; and then the slow commonplace Swiss talk, and the Baumgarten coming in—it is just too glorious! How fresh, how powerful, how exciting! We have no such work as this in music, and yet even that sphere ought one day to produce something equally perfect.[61]

61. Letter to his Family, Engelberg, August 23, 1831.

For the first time in over a year, I saw a German aesthetic paper. The German Parnassus seems in as disorganized a condition as European politics. God help us! I was obliged to swallow the supercilious Menzel, who presumed modesty to depreciate Goethe, and the supercilious Grabbe, who modestly depreciates Shakespeare, and the philosophers who proclaim Schiller to be rather trivial! Is this new, arrogant, overbearing spirit, this perverse cynicism, as odious to you as it is to me?[62]

62. Letter to Wilhelm Taubert, Lucerne, August 27, 1831.

1834

I am well and happy ... and also diligent and working hard at many things. I really believe that Jean Paul, whom I am at this moment reading with intense delight, has also some influence in the matter, for he invariably infects me for at least half a year with his strange peculiarities.[63]

63. Letter to Karl Klingemann, Düsseldorf, December 16, 1834.

1838

I am reading Lessing just now frequently, with true enjoyment and gratitude. At the end of the most fatiguing day, this famous fellow makes me feel quite fresh again.[64]

64. Letter to his Family, Leipzig, November 5, 1838.

1841

For Heaven's sake, tell me, how came you to be reading that abominable thing of Diderot's? He was ashamed of it later in life, but the traces of his genius are to be discovered even in this muddy pool. I may possibly feel more mildly disposed towards him just now, because two pietistic works were sent to me yesterday from Berlin, so gloomy, such a perfect type of the worst time of the priesthood, that I am almost inclined to welcome the French with their audacity and Voltaire with his broom. Perhaps you know one of these? It is called, "Die Passion, ein kirchliches Festspiel"; it is written in doggerel rhymes, and is the most wretched trash I have lately read,—Heine included.[65]

65. Letter to his Brother, Paul, Leipzig, January 2, 1841.

Chapter Fourteen

Mendelssohn on his Daily and Professional Life

1829

On my arrival in London I resumed my quiet life, which consists of composing and reading English.[1]

1. Letter to his Sisters, London, September 10, 1829.

1830

When I come into the room early in the morning, and see the sun shining so brightly on my breakfast, I immediately feel thoroughly comfortable; for it is now far on in the autumn, and who, in our country, can still expect warmth, or a bright sky, or grapes and flowers? After breakfast I begin my work, and play, and sing, and compose till about noon. Then Rome in all her vastness lies before me like a problem in enjoyment; but I go deliberately to work, selecting a different historical object every day. When I am at my morning work I dislike leaving off, and wish to continue my writing, but I say to myself: you must also see the Vatican; and when I once get there, it is just as hard to leave again; thus each of my occupations gives me the purest pleasure, and one enjoyment follows on the heels of the last.[2]

2. Letter to his Parents, Rome, November 8, 1830.

1831

Every morning I have to write, correct and score till one o'clock, when I go to Scheidel's coffee-house in the Kaufinger Gasse and where I know each face by heart, and find the same people every day in the same position: two playing chess, three looking on, five reading the newspapers, six eating their dinner, and I am the seventh. After dinner Baermann usually comes to fetch me and we make arrangements about the concert, or after a walk we have cheese and beer, and then I return home and set to work again. This time I have declined all invitations for the evening; but there are so many agreeable houses to which I may go uninvited, that a light is seldom to be seen in my room on the ground floor till after eight o'clock. You must know that I lodge on a level with the street, in a room which was once a shop, so that if I unbar the shutters of my glass door, one step brings me into the middle of the street and anyone passing along can put his head in at the window, and say good morning.[3]

3. Letter to his Family, Munich, October 6, 1831.

Last Wednesday we had capital fun; several wagers had been won, and it was agreed that we should enjoy the fruits of them all together; and after various suggestions, we at last decided on having a musical soiree in my room, and inviting all the dignitaries. So a list of about thirty people was made out; several also came uninvited, who were presented to us by mutual friends. There was a great lack of space—at first we tried to seat several people on my bed—but a number of patient sheep managed to cram into my small room. The whole affair was extremely lively and successful. First I played my old quartet in B minor; then Breiting sang "Adelaide"; Mr. S played variations on the violin (doing himself no credit); Baermann performed Beethoven's first quartet, which we had arranged for two clarinets, corno di bassetto, and bassoon; an aria from "Euryanthe" followed, which was furiously encored, and as a finale I extemporized—I did not want to—but they made such a tremendous uproar that I was forced to comply through I had nothing in my head but wine-glasses, benches, cold cuts, and ham. When at last the time for eating and drinking arrived, everybody went crazy; we fraternized, glass in hand, and gave toasts; the more formal guests, with their grave faces, sat in the midst of the jovial throng, apparently quite contented, and we did not separate till half-past one in the morning.[4]

4. Letter to his Family, Munich, October 6, 1831.

1832

For the next few years I aspire as little to [a position in the Singakademie, Leipzig] as any other situation; my purpose is to live by what I compose, just as I do here, and I want to be independent. I certainly do not need to convince them of my ability to fill the office; and I neither will, nor can, intrigue.[5]

5. Letter to his Father, Norwood, May 22, 1832.

My room is in order, the pictures are hung, Sebastian Bach over the Piano ... and Rebecca's portrait side by side with Beethoven and a couple of Raphaels—so the walls are rather a medley. I also have a toilet table and on it stands a bottle of Eau de Cologne in its basket, which is particularly admired by all my aunts and my cousins, my three little travel diaries, several wallets, my sketch-books and my old paintbox with a couple of half-finished colored landscapes, on which I should like to work now. On the other side of the room is my old wretched piano without strings which you certainly remember. I have just played my new song on it, *"Sie wandelt im Blumengarten."* Then there is a chest with old letters in which I found one that you sent me to Hamburg in April, 1829, and which begins with, "it is a great and good thing that you are coming!"; and many potted plants, books, tables, several chairs and a lot of dust on the floor. And if by now you do not know what my place is like, it is not my fault.[6]

6. Letter to Karl Klingemann, Berlin, July 4, 1832.

1833

Even though I have become convinced that Berlin society is an awful monster, I should like to remain here some time longer. I feel comfortable, and find it rather difficult to set out traveling again. All the morning there is a constant knocking at my door, but I do not open, and am happy to think what bores I may have escaped, unknown to myself.[7]

7. Letter to Ignaz Moscheles, Berlin, March 17, 1833.

1834

I feel particularly comfortable in this place, having just as much official occupation as I want and like, and plenty of time for myself. When I do not feel inclined to compose, there is conducting and rehearsing, and it is quite a pleasure to see how well and brightly things go. There is an opera, a choral society, an orchestra, church music, a public, and even a small opposition; it is simply delightful.[8]

8. Letter to Ignaz Moscheles, Düsseldorf, February 7, 1834.

One of my Düsseldorf troubles is at this moment beginning; I mean my next door neighbor, who has placed her piano against the wall just on the other side of mine, and to my sorrow practices two hours a day, making every day the same mistakes, and playing all Rossini's arias in such a desperately slow, phlegmatic tempo, that I certainly must have played her some malicious trick, had it not occurred to me that she was probably at all hours more tormented by my piano than I by hers. Then I sometimes hear the teacher or the mother (I can't tell which) strike the right note distinctly seventeen times in succession; and when she is playing at sight, and gradually out of the darkness develops some old barrel-organ tune, which could be recognized by a single note,—it is hard to bear.[9]

9. Letter to his Sister, Fanny, Düsseldorf, April 7, 1834.

When I sat down to my work in the morning, at every bar there was a ringing at the bell; then came grumbling choristers to be snubbed, stupid singers to be taught, seedy musicians to be engaged; and when this had gone on the whole day, and I felt that all these things were for the whole benefit and advantage of the Düsseldorf theater, I was provoked; at last, two days ago, I made a *salto mortale*, and beat a retreat out of the whole affair, and once more feel myself a man. This resignation was a very unpleasant piece of intelligence for our theatrical autocrat, *alias* stage mufti; he compressed his lips viciously, as if he would fain eat me up; however, I made a short and very eloquent speech to the Director, in which I spoke of my own avocations as being of more consequence to me than the Düsseldorf theater, much as I, etc ... In short, they let me off, on condition that I would occasionally conduct; this I promised, and this I will certainly perform.[10]

10. Letter to his Mother, Düsseldorf, November 4, 1834.

The Intendant proposed that I should be the musical intendant, and he the theatrical intendant. Then the question arose, which was to take precedence. We exchanged desperately uncivil letters. We came to an agreement after this, but quarreled again immediately, for he required me to go to Aix, to hear and to engage a singer there, and this I did not choose to do. Then I was desired to engage an orchestra,—that is, prepare two contracts for each member, and previously fight to the death about a dollar more or less of their monthly salary; then they went away, then they came back and signed all the same, then they all objected to sit at the second music desk, then came the aunt of a very wretched performer, whom I could not engage, and the wife and two little children of another miserable musician, to intercede with the Director; then I allowed three fellows to play on trial, and they played so utterly beneath contempt that I really could not agree to take any of them; then they looked very humble, and went quietly away, very miserable, having lost their daily bread; then came the wife again, and wept. Out of thirty persons there was only one who said at once, "I am satisfied," and signed his contract; all the others bargained and haggled for an hour at least, before I could make them understand that I had a *prix fixé* ... they were four of the most disagreeable days I ever passed. On the fourth, Klingemann arrived in the morning, saw the state of things, and was horrified. In the mean time Rietz studied the "Templar," morning and evening; the choruses got drunk, and I was forced to speak with authority; then they rebelled against the manager, and I was obliged to shout at them like the Boots at an inn.[11]

11. Letter to his Sister Rebecca, Düsseldorf, November 23, 1834.

1835

Today I rode through the forest, and stopped for at least a quarter of an hour to listen to the birds.[12]

12. Letter to his Father, Düsseldorf, April 3, 1835.

The day before yesterday my Leipzig music-directorship commenced. I cannot tell you how much I am satisfied with this beginning, and with the whole aspect of my position here. It is a quiet, regular, official business. That the Institute has been established for fifty-six years is very perceptible, and moreover the people seem most friendly and well-disposed towards me and my music. The orchestra is very good, and thoroughly musical; and I think that six months hence it will be much improved, for the sympathy and attention with which these people receive my suggestions, and instantly adopt them, were really touching in both the rehearsals we have hitherto had; there was as great a difference as if another orchestra had been playing. There are still some deficiencies in the orchestra, but these will be supplied by degrees; and I look forward to a succession of pleasant evenings and good performances.[13]

13. Letter to his Family, Leipzig, October 6, 1835.

1836

My position here is of the most agreeable nature,—cordial people, a good orchestra, the most susceptible and grateful musical public; only just as much work to do as I like, and an opportunity of hearing my new compositions at once. I have plenty of pleasant society besides, so that this would indeed seem to be all that was required to constitute happiness, were it not deeper seated![14]

I am now fairly established in Germany, and shall not require to make a pilgrimage into foreign countries to secure my existence. This, indeed, has only been evident during the last year, and since my being placed at Leipzig; but now I have no longer any doubts on the subject, and think there is no lack of modesty in rejoicing at the fact.[15]

I came here with plans for great industry, but for nearly a week I have done little else every forenoon but admire the view and sun myself. I must go on in the same way for a couple of days more—idleness is so pleasant, and agrees with me so well.[16]

1837

I have worked a good deal lately, and mean to be still more industrious.[17]

1838

I am pretty well settled here now for the next two or three years; it suits me very well, for I have only the twenty concerts in the winter, and all the time between and the whole summer quite free; then I have a delightful apartment with an extensive view over the fields, and there I live and compose to my heart's content.[18]

1839

I have so little time to myself in the winter. The concerts and the whole way of life take up more time and leisure than I expected, and I am glad enough if in my spare time I can just manage to clear up my unfinished work, leaving new things to be begun in the summer months.[19]

1840

I am living here in as complete quiet and solitude as I could possibly desire; thanks be to God, my wife and children are

14. Letter to Frederick Rosen, Leipzig, February 6, 1836.

15. Letter to his Mother, Düsseldorf, June 1, 1836.

16. Letter to his Family, Frankfurt, July 14, 1836.

17. Letter to Ignaz Moscheles, Speier, April 6, 1837.

18. Letter to Madame Kiene, Leipzig, February 24, 1838.

19. Letter to Anton Zuccalmaglio, Leipzig, December 4, 1839.

well, I have plenty of work, and what more can man desire? I do not ask Heaven to grant me anything else and I start every day by enjoying anew my peaceful and monotonous life. I admit that at the beginning of the winter I generally have difficulty avoiding the somewhat philistine social gatherings which bloom and thrive here and in which one might be enticed to participate and thus lose much time and pleasure. By now I have pretty well succeeded in getting rid of them.[20]

20. Letter to Karl Klingemann, Leipzig, November 18, 1840.

Massow mentions the salary, the direction of the classes, and the concerts to be given by royal command, but without entering into any further particulars. There was but one obstacle in the way, which was, that I did not precisely know what was expected from me in return for such a proposal. I then brought under his notice the difficulties opposed to a *bona fide* direction of the present classes; and as he had mentioned that these would not now occupy much of my time, but that it was expected I should, under the new system, undertake additional work, I begged, therefore, at least to be told what were the limits of this system, and the duties I had to perform; that I was indeed quite willing to work, but did not choose to pledge myself to the performance of functions that were not precisely defined. With regard to the concerts, I told him my opinion as to the only mode of arranging them now in Berlin; that little good could accrue from merely occasional performances, even by royal command; for in that case all sorts of counter-influences would have full scope; that an institute must be founded exclusively for similar concerts, and likewise days fixed for the rehearsals and concerts, and the instruction of the performers, etc.; that I would have nothing to do with the orchestra, except on *this* condition, that I was to be absolute director-in-chief of these concerts, etc.[21]

21. Letter to his Brother, Paul, Leipzig, December 20, 1840, regarding a possible position at the court in Berlin.

1841

I told Massow in a letter today that I should be happy to explain my views with regard to reorganizing the Musical Academy; for this purpose he has only to send me the statutes hitherto in force, and the composition of the classes, of which I am entirely ignorant, and also say how far the modifications are to be carried, whether to the extent of a radical change, or merely a reform; this I must learn, of course, or I should not know what to say. It sounds all so different from what they commissioned you to say to me when you came here; and if it begins in such a way, no doubt the sequel will be still worse. The salary they offer is certainly handsome and liberal, but if they in return expect me to accept an unlimited obligation to work, that also would be a change in their proposals, and no compensation to me. The salary is the only point on which Massow spoke in a decided manner to me, and my position is too fortunate for mere money to influence my views. All that you told me here about a rotation between the different directors, and the duties of the Kapellmeister of the Royal Chapel, and of the engagement of other foreign musicians,— not a word of this was brought forward; on the contrary, Massow writes to me that he is glad I have declared myself satisfied with the title and the salary, which is totally opposed to the sense of my previous letter, in which I expressed a wish to know my duties before I could explain my intentions. Indeed, even if the alteration in the musical class were to be entered into, and carried through exactly according to my wishes, I scarcely know whether I should quite like to go to Berlin as "Director of the Musical Class" which is by no means in good odor with musicians at present. I can say all this to you without incurring the suspicion of a fondness for titles, for what annoys me is their drawing back in all their proposals.[22]

22. Letter to his Brother, Paul, Leipzig, January 2, 1841.

This is the thirty-fifth letter I have written since the day before yesterday. Who can give me back the precious days which pass away in these things? Add to this, persons who wish to be examined, eagerly awaiting my report for their anxious relatives, whether they are to become professional musicians or not; two Rhenish youths are here at this moment for that purpose, and the verdict is to be given in the course of a few hours. It is really a heavy responsibility, and I often think of La Fontaine's rat, who retired into a cheese and thence delivered oracles.[23]

23. Letter to his Mother, Leipzig, January 25, 1841.

I still have misgivings as to Berlin being a soil where a person of my profession could feel even tolerably at home, in spite of all the honors and money; but the mere offer in itself gives me an inward impulse, a certain satisfaction, which is of infinite value to me, even if I were never to speak of it to anyone; in a word, I feel that an honor has been done me, and I rejoice in it.[24]

I have conducted fifteen public performances since January, enough to knock up any man.[25]

Since January we have been having an uninterrupted succession of musical events, besides which the Leipzigers are so very sociable that at this time one is hardly allowed a quiet evening at home. Our own house has become a lively center too. We invite our friends and they return the compliment. We speak German, French, and English all in one breath; and all the while the orchestra is fiddling, trumpeting, and drumming every day, whilst one is expected to sit an hour and a half at supper, and sing four-part songs to a roast beef accompaniment.[26]

I am off for a year to Berlin, one of the sourest apples a man can eat, and yet eaten it must be. That I am now to recommence a private life, but at the same time to become a sort of schoolmaster to a Conservatorium, is what I can scarcely understand, after my excellent vigorous orchestra here. I might perhaps do so if I were really to enjoy an entirely private life, in which case I should only compose and live in retirement; but the mongrel Berlin doings interfere,—the vast projects, the petty execution, the admirable criticism, the indifferent musicians, the liberal ideas, the Court officials in the streets, the Museum and the Academy, and the sand! I doubt whether my stay there will be more than a year.[27]

I have begun a big symphony, and am all ready in the third movement, and work at it every day with delight; I also continue my sketching, drink mineral water which agrees with me splendidly, and spend the evenings happily with my family.[28]

1842

What with eating, drinking, walking, sketching, enjoying myself, and not caring for the morrow, I have not been able to write anything new.[29]

24. Letter to his Brother, Paul, Leipzig, February 13, 1841.

25. Letter to Julius Schubring, Leipzig, February 27, 1841.

26. Letter to Charlotte Moscheles, Leipzig, March 14, 1841.

27. Letter to Karl Klingemann, Leipzig, July 15, 1841.

28. Letter to Karl Klingemann, Berlin, September 6, 1841.

29. Letter to Charlotte Moscheles, Berlin, October 8, 1842.

The music school here, please God! will make a beginning next February; Hauptmann, David, Schumann and his wife, Becker, Pohlenz and I, are to be the teachers at first. Ten scholars are received gratis; the rest who may wish to have instruction must pay seventy-five thalers a year.[30]

30. Letter to his Mother, Leipzig, December 11, 1842.

1843

My winter months are so completely filled up with work, both public and private, that I do not have the least time for social intercourse.[31]

31. Letter to an undesignated person, Leipzig, April 2, 1843.

Herr von Massow has sent me a communication connected with that tedious everlasting affair, which irritated me so much that it almost made me ill, and I do not feel right yet. Instead of receiving the assent to the proposals on which we had agreed in the interview of the 10th, Herr von Massow sends me a commission to arrange for orchestra and chorus, without delay, the chorale, *"Herr Gott, Dich loben wir,"* the longest chorale and the most tiresome work which I ever attempted; and the day after I had finished it and sent it off, I receive an official document which I must sign before the assent of the King can be solicited; when I had signed it, the others present at that conference would also subscribe their names. In this deed all the stipulations are correctly stated, but six or eight additional clauses are written on the margin not one syllable of which had ever been named during the conference, invalidating the whole intention of the above stipulations, and placing myself and the Institute in the most entire subservience to Herr von Kustner. After two days consideration I therefore wrote to Herr von Massow, why and wherefore I could not give my signature, requesting him to inform me whether the King intended to carry out our former agreement. If he did not feel disposed to do so, or if he, Herr von Massow, considered it necessary to insert new clauses in the agreement, I should then consider the affair impracticable, and must act accordingly. I assure you that the affair cost me four most angry, disturbed, and irksome days. All might be smoothed over and set to rights by a few words, and every moment I expect to hear them spoken, and then there would be a possibility of something good and new; but they are not spoken, and they are replaced by a thousand annoyances, and my head at last is so bewildered that I think I become almost as perverted and unnatural as the whole affair is at last likely to turn out.[32]

32. Letter to his Brother, Paul, Leipzig, July 21, 1843.

1844

I will always obey the commands of a sovereign so beloved by me, even at the sacrifice of my personal wishes and advantage. If I find I cannot do so with a *good artistic conscience,* I must endeavor candidly to state my scruples or my incapacity, and if that does not suffice, then I must go. This may sound absurd in the mouth of a musician, but shall I not feel duty as much in *my* position as others do in *theirs*? In an occurrence so personally important to me, shall I not follow the dictates of integrity and truth, as I have striven to do all my life?[33]

33. Letter to Wirklich Geheimrath Bunsen, Frankfurt, May 4, 1844.

I decline taking the other hint,—as to making a present to the leading performers. This would be contrary to the fixed principles which I adopted at the beginning of my musical career,—never in any way to mix up my personal position with my musical one, or ever to improve the latter by the influence of the former, or in any manner to bribe public or private opinion with regard to me, or even attempt to strengthen it.[34]

34. Letter to Julius Stern, London, May 27, 1844.

We have early strawberries for breakfast, at two we dine, have supper at half-past eight in the evening, and by ten we are all asleep.[35]

35. Letter to Carl Klingemann, Frankfurt, July 17, 1844.

If I could only continue to live during half a year as I have done here for a fortnight past, what might I not accomplish? But the regulation and direction of so many concerts, and attending others, is no joke, and nothing is gained by it.[36]

36. Letter to his Sister, Fanny, Soden, August 15, 1844.

My position here has been modified during the last few days quite according to my wishes. I shall continue to stand in relations with the king as a composer, for which I shall receive a moderate salary, but of all connection with public performances here, and necessary residence in Berlin, which have so long tormented and weighed upon me, I am happily quit.[37]

37. Letter to Eduard Devrient, Berlin, October 25, 1844.

1847

My wife and children are well, God be praised! We walk a great deal, the children do their lessons, Cecile paints Alpine roses, and I write music: so the days pass monotonously and quickly.[38]

38. Letter to General von Webern, Interlachen, August 15, 1847.

About the author

David Whitwell is a graduate ("with distinction") of the University of Michigan and the Catholic University of America, Washington D.C. (Ph.D., Musicology, Distinguished Alumni Award, 2000) and has studied conducting with Eugene Ormandy and at the Akademie für Musik, Vienna. Prior to coming to Northridge, Dr. Whitwell participated in concerts throughout the United States and Asia as Associate First Horn in the USAF Band and Orchestra in Washington, D.C., and in recitals throughout South America in cooperation with the United States State Department.

At the California State University, Northridge, which is in Los Angeles, Dr. Whitwell developed the CSUN Wind Ensemble into an ensemble of international reputation, with international tours to Europe in 1981 and 1989 and to Japan in 1984. The CSUN Wind Ensemble has made professional studio recordings for BBC (London), the Köln Westdeutscher Rundfunk (Germany), NOS National Radio (The Netherlands), Zürich Radio (Switzerland), the Television Broadcasting System (Japan) as well as for the United States State Department for broadcast on its "Voice of America" program. The CSUN Wind Ensemble's recording with the Mirecourt Trio in 1982 was named the "Record of the Year" by The Village Voice. Composers who have guest conducted Whitwell's ensembles include Aaron Copland, Ernest Krenek, Alan Hovhaness, Morton Gould, Karel Husa, Frank Erickson and Vaclav Nelhybel.

Dr. Whitwell has been a guest professor in 100 different universities and conservatories throughout the United States and in 23 foreign countries (most recently in China, in an elite school housed in the Forbidden City). Guest conducting experiences have included the Philadelphia Orchestra, Seattle Symphony Orchestra, the Czech Radio Orchestras of Brno and Bratislava, The National Youth Orchestra of Israel, as well as resident wind ensembles in Russia, Israel, Austria, Switzerland, Germany, England, Wales, The Netherlands, Portugal, Peru, Korea, Japan, Taiwan, Canada and the United States.

He is a past president of the College Band Directors National Association, a member of the Prasidium of the International Society for the Promotion of Band Music, and was a member of the founding board of directors of the World Association for Symphonic Bands and Ensembles (WASBE). In 1964 he was made an honorary life member of Kappa Kappa Psi, a national professional music fraternity. In September, 2001, he was a delegate to the UNESCO Conference on Global Music in Tokyo. He has been knighted by sovereign organizations in France, Portugal and Scotland and has been awarded the gold medal of Kerkrade, The Netherlands, and the silver medal of Wangen, Germany, the highest honor given wind conductors in the United States, the medal of the Academy of Wind and Percussion Arts (National Band Association) and the highest honor given wind conductors in Austria, the gold medal of the Austrian Band Association. He is a member of the Hall of Fame of the California Music Educators Association.

Dr. Whitwell's publications include more than 127 articles on wind literature including publications in Music and Letters (London), the London Musical Times, the Mozart-Jahrbuch (Salzburg), and 39 books, among which is his 13-volume History and Literature of the Wind Band Ensemble and an 8-volume series on Aesthetics in Music. In addition to numerous modern editions of early wind band music his original compositions include 5 symphonies.

David Whitwell was named as one of six men who have determined the course of American bands during the second half of the 20th century, in the definitive history, The Twentieth Century American Wind Band (Meredith Music).

A doctoral dissertation by German Gonzales (2007, Arizona State University) is dedicated to the life and conducting career of David Whitwell through the year 1977. David Whitwell is one of nine men described by Paula A. Crider in The Conductor's Legacy (Chicago: GIA, 2010) as "the legendary conductors" of the 20th century.

"I can't imagine the 2nd half of the 20th century—without David Whitwell and what he has given to all of the rest of us."
Frederick Fennell (1993)

www.ingramcontent.com/pod-product-compliance
Lightning Source LLC
Chambersburg PA
CBHW080450170426
43196CB00016B/2753